THE DREAM IS ALIVE

A FLIGHT OF DISCOVERY ABOARD THE SPACE SHUTTLE · Written by Barbara Embury

in consultation with Tom D. Crouch, Ph.D.
Chairman, Department of Aeronautics, Smithsonian Institution

A Somerville House Book
Harper & Row, Publishers

This book is based on the film The Dream Is Alive, *funded by Lockheed Corporation and the Smithsonian Institution's National Air and Space Museum, in co-operation with the National Aeronautics and Space Administration.*

Text and Illustration Compilation Copyright © 1990 Somerville House Books Ltd.
Text Copyright © 1990 Barbara Embury.

IMAX® photographs from the film *The Dream Is Alive* Copyright © 1985 Lockheed Corporation and Smithsonian Institution.
Smithsonian / National Air and Space Museum photographs Copyright © 1990 Smithsonian Institution.

Embury, Barbara.
    The dream is alive / Barbara Embury, with Thomas D. Crouch.
    p.   cm – (IMAX®/ Smithsonian wide world series)
    "A Somerville House Book."
    Summary: Describes the experiences of those who ride in the NASA space shuttle.
    ISBN-0-06-021813-4   ISBN-0-06-021814-2 (lib. bdg.)
    1. Space shuttles – Juvenile literature. 2. Space flight.)   I. Crouch,
    Tom D.   II. Title.   III. Series.
    RL795.5.E44   1990
    629. 45 – dc20   90-55194
                                                      CIP
                                                      AC

Library of Congress. Catalog Number: 90-55194
1 2 3 4 5 6 7 8 9 10
First Edition

Harper & Row Junior Books
10 East 53rd Street
New York, NY 10022

Produced by Somerville House Books Ltd.

With special thanks for the co-operation of the Book Development Division of the Smithsonian Institution Press.

IMAX® is a registered trademark of Imax Systems Corporation, 38 Isabella Street, Toronto, Ontario, M4Y 1N1.

Designed by Andrew Smith and Annabelle Stanley / Andrew Smith Graphics Inc.
Illustrations by Jack McMaster

Smithsonian picture research by Paula Ballo-Dailey
Educational consultant: Penny Fine

Although the book is based on these specific missions, the information about the shuttle program is up-to-date and applies generally to all current missions.

Mission 41C Apr. 6 – 13, 1984
Crew:
Commander - Robert Crippen
Pilot - Francis (Dick) Scobee
Mission Specialists - Terry Hart, George Nelson, James van Hoften
Orbiter: *Challenger*
   This was the mission that rescued and repaired the Solar Max satellite.

Mission 41D Aug. 30 – Sept. 5, 1984
Crew:
Commander - Henry Hartsfield
Pilot - Michael Coats
Mission Specialists - Judith Resnik, Richard Mullane, Steven Hawley
Payload Specialist - Charles Walker
Orbiter: *Discovery*
   This was *Discovery*'s maiden flight, the mission that unfurled the solar-array panel.

Mission 41G Oct. 5 – Oct. 13, 1984
Crew:
Commander - Robert Crippen
Pilot - Jon McBride
Mission Specialists - Sally Ride, Kathryn Sullivan, David Leestma
Payload Specialists - Marc Garneau, Paul Scully-Power
Orbiter: *Challenger*
   The launch and landing of this mission are described in this book. This was the mission on which Sullivan and Leestma took a space walk.

Opposite page: Italy seen from the windows of the shuttle orbiter, about 280 miles (450 kilometers) above the Earth.

Front cover: Against a backdrop of planet Earth, astronauts work in the weightlessness of space in the cargo bay of the shuttle's orbiter.

Title page: A daytime shuttle launch from the Kennedy Space Center on the Atlantic coast of Florida. In the lower right corner you can see the huge Vehicle Assembly Building, where the main parts of the shuttle are put together.

Back cover: IMAX theater viewers share the experience of space with astronauts in the film The Dream Is Alive.

CONTENTS

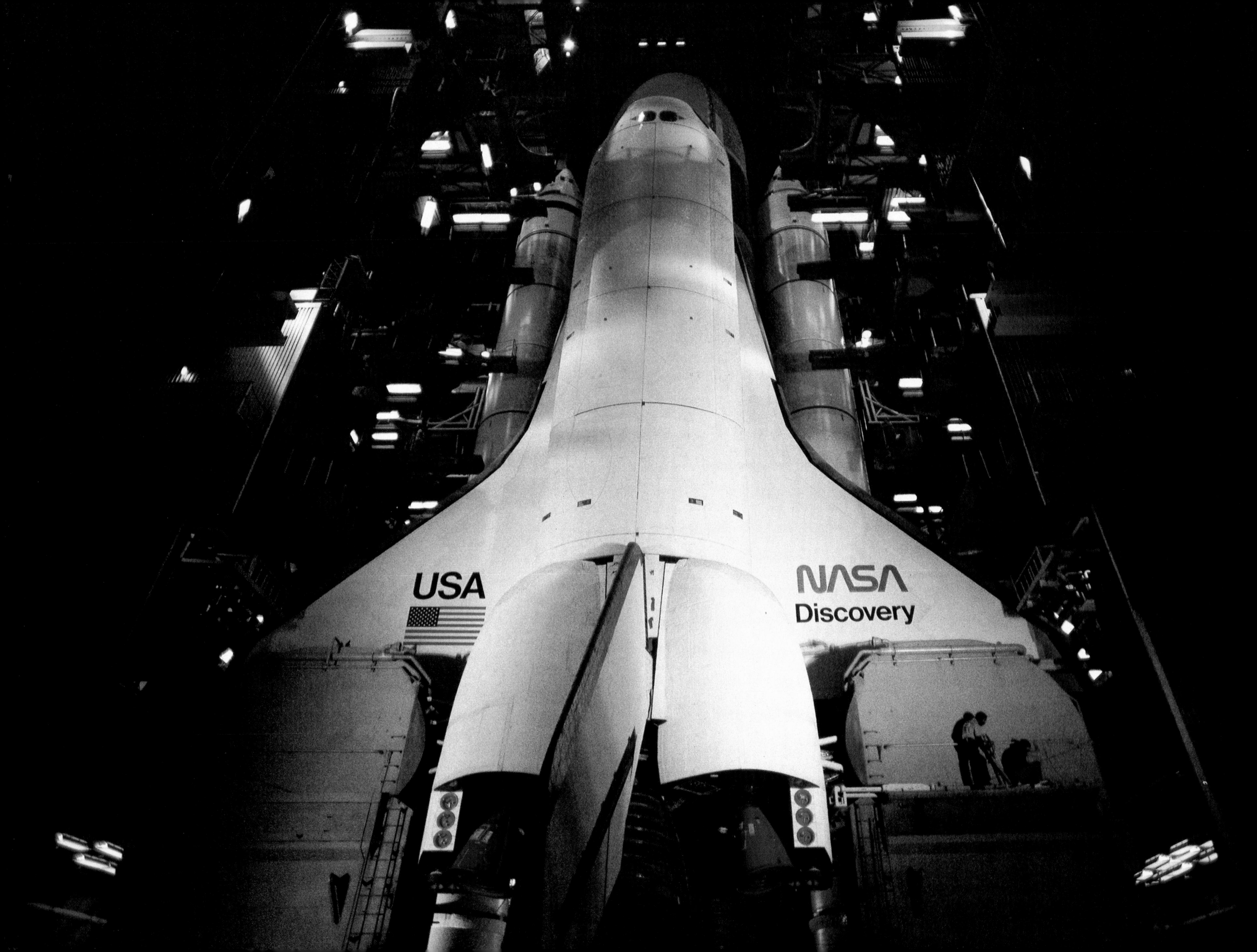
USA
NASA
Discovery

RIDING A COLUMN OF FIRE

For the seven men and women who will ride the shuttle on Mission 41G, launch day starts well before dawn. But no one complains about the early hour. This is the day they've waited for, through all their long months of training. There's time for breakfast – their last Earth meal for a week. Then the shuttle astronauts, in their light-blue flight suits, smile and wave to photographers before climbing into the van that will take them to the launchpad.

All around them are reminders of the pioneers who went before. From this place, the Kennedy Space Center, the first American rocketed into space in 1961. Just eight years later three men left here on a journey to the moon. This is a place where people have always accepted the challenge and the risk of space exploration. And now it's the turn of the Mission 41G astronauts to write a page of space history.

It's the first time an American woman – Mission Specialist Sally Ride – will make a second trip into space, and the first time a second woman – Mission Specialist Kathryn Sullivan – will be aboard. Sullivan, if all goes well, will become the first American woman to take a walk in space, along with Mission Specialist David Leestma. Payload Specialist Marc Garneau is about to become the first Canadian in space, and the other payload specialist, Paul Scully-Power, a U.S. citizen, will be the first Australian-born astronaut.

Although it is still dark, the launchpad is drenched in light from powerful floodlights. The looming shuttle, taller than a thirty-story building, groans and gurgles as it comes to life for another trip into space. It's 2 hours to "T minus zero" – the moment (Time) of lift-off.

At T minus 5 hours, while the crew was still asleep, a team of technicians entered the shuttle orbiter for one last check. The orbiter, which looks like a passenger jet, is the part of the shuttle where the astronauts ride,

THE SHUTTLE

External Fuel Tank

Solid Rocket Boosters

Orbital Maneuvering System (OMS) Engines

Orbiter

USA

Main Engines

Above: *Jules Verne's novel* From the Earth to the Moon *told of an imaginary journey to the moon in a shell fired from a giant cannon. The book was first published in 1865, 104 years before the first human beings actually landed on the moon.*

Opposite page: *In the Vehicle Assembly Building, the orbiter* Discovery *is "mated" to two solid rocket boosters. After the towering external fuel tank has been added, the shuttle will be ready to roll out to the launchpad.*

SALLY KRISTEN RIDE
Born Los Angeles, California, May 26, 1951

Sally Ride was in the first group of six women who were accepted into the space program in 1978. When the National Aeronautics and Space Administration (NASA) later announced that Ride would be the first American woman in space, she got a lot of media attention. "It's too bad this is such a big deal," said Ride. "It's time that people realize women can do any job they want to do."

Ride thought about a lot of different careers while she was growing up, but being an astronaut wasn't one of them. In those days American space-flight was for men only. In high school Ride was the 18th-ranked junior tennis player in the United States, and she briefly considered turning professional. Later, she planned to be a college physics professor.

The space program made good use of Ride's science background. And as it turned out, all those long hours of trying to put the tennis ball exactly where she wanted it came in handy too! One of Ride's specialties became operating the shuttle's robotic arm. Her concentration and excellent hand-eye coordination soon made her an expert. "It got to be as natural as using tweezers on a noodle," she said.

Ride was the first astronaut to use the arm for space work, including satellite deployments. On her first flight in June 1983 and on a second flight in 1984, Ride – and the arm – performed flawlessly.

Ride became known for her imaginative use of the arm, such as the gentle shaking of a satellite to loosen some solar panels that refused to unfold. During Mission 41D, when Ride was providing ground support, a dangerous icicle formed on the outside of the orbiter. The mission astronauts needed advice: Could the arm be maneuvered to knock off the ice? If not, two astronauts – including Ride's husband, Steven Hawley – would have to go on an unscheduled space walk to deal with it. Ride and three other astronauts stayed up all night working on the problem and figured out how the arm could do the job – and it worked!

and the part that is used again for other missions. A lot of fuel is needed to get the orbiter into orbit. By T minus 4 hours the huge, orange external fuel tank was being filled with 143,000 U.S. gallons (541,000 liters) of liquid oxygen and over 385,000 U.S. gallons (1.45 million liters) of liquid hydrogen. During the first few minutes after launch, the three main orbiter engines will guzzle this fuel at the rate of 64,000 U.S. gallons (242,000 liters) per minute.

As the astronauts ride up in an elevator to board the orbiter, they can smell the salty tang of the coastal Florida air. Technicians help them on with their launch helmets, which will give them oxygen and radio communications during lift-off. Then the crew members crawl through a side hatch in the orbiter and take their seats. Because the orbiter is standing on end, the astronauts have to lie on their backs in their seats while they wait for lift-off. Commander Robert Crippen and Pilot Jon McBride (who function like the pilot and copilot of an airplane) are side by side on the flight deck. Two mission specialists are seated behind them. The third mission specialist and the two payload specialists are strapped into seats on the mid deck.

At the launch control center about 200 people are sitting in front of computer screens, monitoring all the shuttle's systems. Computers carry out every

Opposite page: The moment of lift-off. Three powerful main engines and two solid rocket boosters propel the shuttle, which weighs 4.4 million pounds (2 million kilograms) when it is launched.

LAUNCHING THE SHUTTLE

1. The main engines and the solid rocket boosters fire and the shuttle lifts off. About 3 seconds later, the shuttle clears the tower.

2. At 2 minutes into the flight, the solid rocket boosters are empty of fuel. They separate from the orbiter and fall to the Atlantic Ocean on parachutes.

3. At 8 1/2 minutes into the flight, the external tank has fed all its fuel into the orbiter's engines. The empty tank separates from the orbiter. As it falls back into the Earth's atmosphere, it breaks up into small pieces which plummet into the ocean.

4. About 2 minutes later, the orbiter's Orbital Maneuvering System (OMS) engines fire to send the orbiter into orbit around the Earth.

Above: As the shuttle safely clears the tower, launch control erupts with joy and relief.

Opposite page: *Seconds into its maiden voyage on Mission 41D,* Discovery *is about to clear the tower.*

important step in the launch, although people make the final decisions about whether it is safe for the shuttle to lift off.

At T minus 1 hour, the hatch door on the orbiter is closed and locked. The technicians drive off to a safe spot several miles away from the launchpad. Now the astronauts are alone in the shuttle.

Commander Crippen is the most experienced of all shuttle pilots, with three shuttle missions behind

THE TRAGEDY OF *CHALLENGER*
January 28, 1986

If we feared danger, mankind would never go into space – Ellison Onizuka

No one who saw the explosion will ever forget the sight. Just 73 seconds into its tenth launch, a great orange and white fireball engulfed the space shuttle *Challenger*. The solid rocket boosters tore away from the orbiter and traced a giant double arch of flame in the bright blue sky. Trailing plumes of smoke, pieces of the orbiter fell toward the sea. All seven people aboard – Francis (Dick) Scobee, Michael Smith, Ellison Onizuka, Judith Resnik, Ronald McNair, Gregory Jarvis and Christa McAuliffe – were killed.

The Rogers Commission to investigate the *Challenger* explosion had thirteen members, including Sally Ride, the first American woman in space, and Neil Armstrong, the first person on the moon. After four months of hearing expert evidence, the Commission issued a report in October 1986. The report said that an "O" ring – a rubber pressure seal – on the right solid rocket booster probably had failed. A jet of flame and searing gas from this leaking joint broke the connection between the booster and the rest of the shuttle. As it broke off, the booster smashed a hole in the external fuel tank, which contained thousands of gallons of liquid hydrogen and oxygen. When the fuel tank exploded, it blew *Challenger* apart. The report also said that warnings had been ignored that the shuttle was unsafe. The shuttle program shut down for more than two years, while hundreds of design changes were made. A crew escape system was added to the orbiter, the main engines were made stronger, and a fire detection system was added to the external fuel tank. More than 155 changes were made to the solid rocket booster, including much stronger seals. There were also changes in the way the space program was run, so that NASA management would have to listen to the safety concerns of its employees.

On October 2, 1988, the orbiting astronauts of *Discovery* read a tribute to the *Challenger* crew: "Dear friends, we have resumed the journey that we promised to continue for you ... your spirit and your dreams are still alive in our hearts."

him. Pilot McBride is flying the shuttle for the first time. Only the commander and the pilot have a clear view through the windows of the orbiter. However, they're too busy checking over their instrument panel (which includes three green video displays) and talking to launch control to spend much time admiring the Florida dawn. In the last hour leading up to launch, every system, every switch must be checked, with the help of five on-board computers. Meanwhile, the payload specialists, with nothing to do until the shuttle is in orbit, have a long, tense wait on the cramped mid deck.

Step by step the ties that link the shuttle to Earth are broken. At T minus 7 minutes, the walkway the astronauts used to board the shuttle is pulled away. At T minus 5, the shuttle's own power system switches on. The crew members close the visors on their helmets and begin to breathe from their oxygen supplies.

T minus 1 minute. A gusty sigh of vapor billows out of the orbiter's main engines. T minus 16 seconds. Thousands of gallons of water flood over the launchpad to protect it from the tremendous waves of sound and heat that come with lift-off.

Launch control begins the countdown: T minus 10 seconds . . . 9 . . . 8 . . . The three main shuttle engines fire. The shuttle lurches on the launchpad, still attached to the tower. T minus 6 . . . 5 . . . 4 . . . Computers quickly check out the engines and decide whether they're firing properly. If they find anything wrong, the launch can still be stopped.

Opposite page: *A spectacular pre-dawn launch of the shuttle.*

BLAST OFF!

It is believed that the Chinese invented rockets. They may have been using them in battle – with arrows attached – over 700 years ago. Although these weapons were as small and simple as fireworks rockets, they worked in the same way as the rockets that take people into space. Rockets are the only things that exist that can make spacecraft go fast enough to overcome the pull of gravity and leave the Earth behind. But there's another reason rockets are needed for spaceflight. The engines we use on Earth – for automobiles and even jet planes – would be useless in the airlessness of space. The fuel for these engines must be mixed with oxygen from the air before it will burn. But rockets carry their own oxygen supply.

In its simplest form, a rocket is a hollow tube filled with fuel – something that will release gases when it is burned – and an oxidizer – something that will produce oxygen so that the fuel can burn. The top end of the rocket is sealed, and at the bottom end there is a nozzle. When the rocket is lit, the fuel burns rapidly, giving off gases. These gases can escape only through the nozzle in the end of the rocket. As the gases rush downward, the rocket is thrust upward.

Most space rockets have actually been two or more rockets, or stages, stacked on top of each other. The first stage (which is the largest one, on the bottom) pushes the other stages high into the atmosphere, then drops away. After that the second stage ignites and carries the spacecraft farther into space. The Saturn V rocket, which sent 27 Americans on journeys to the moon between 1968 and 1972, was a three-stage liquid-fuel rocket that stood 365 feet (111 meters) tall on the launchpad. It was the largest, most powerful rocket ever launched from our planet.

The space shuttle has two kinds of rockets to take it into orbit. The shuttle uses "parallel staging," which means that all rockets fire at once to lift the shuttle from the Earth. There are two side-by-side rockets attached to the orbiter containing a "solid" mixture of fuel and oxidizer that has the rubbery texture of a pencil eraser. There are also three powerful liquid-fuel rocket engines at the base of the orbiter. Although a mighty Saturn rocket was launched on each Apollo mission, only a nose cone carrying the astronauts came back to Earth after the mission. But the shuttle orbiter and rocket booster casings return home to be used again and again.

Two black powder rockets would have propelled this ancient Chinese weapon.

T minus 3 . . . 2 . . . 1 . . . The solid rocket boosters (SRBs) fire. Now there's no turning back – the rockets can't be shut down. The ground shakes with a deafening rumble as great clouds of smoke and steam billow at the shuttle's base. Then, looking almost sluggish, the shuttle starts to rise.

To break away from Earth, the 4.5-million-pound (2-million-kilogram) shuttle is boosted by a lift-off thrust of 2.6 million pounds (11.8 million newtons) from each of the SRBs, plus more than 1 million pounds (over 5 million newtons) of thrust from the three main engines of the orbiter.

The shuttle clears the tower and rolls over so that the orbiter is on the underside. Then, trailing a column of blinding, white-hot flame 600 feet (200 meters) long, the shuttle lights up the sky as it rises.

For the astronauts it is a bone-rattling ride. Dick Scobee, who was pilot on Mission 41C, said that it was like being on a runaway express train. The shuttle shakes and bangs, and the roar of the engines is almost numbing. Yet the astronauts continue checking their readouts. Over the roar they can still hear the calm voices of ground control through their headphones.

At 2 minutes into flight, the shuttle is already more than 28 miles (45 kilometers) from Earth. The SRBs, which have burned up all their fuel, separate from the orbiter. The empty rocket cases parachute down and are fished out of the Atlantic Ocean about 170 miles (270 kilometers) from the launch site. Tugs tow them back to land so they can be used again.

Opposite page: *The shuttle climbs rapidly after launch.*

Inside the orbiter there's instant relief. With the rocket boosters gone, the ride becomes smooth and quiet. The sky has turned from blue to black as the shuttle continues its climb.

At about 6-1/2 minutes into flight, the shuttle is 80 miles (128 kilometers) from Earth. The astronauts feel as if giant fists are pushing them back against their seats. It's a tiring effort to lift their arms and they have to use their hands to turn their heads. The force of acceleration is now 3 Gs, which means that they feel three times as heavy as they do on Earth. (G forces are the forces bodies experience when they are speeded up quickly or slowed down quickly. "G" stands for gravity. The pull of gravity on Earth is equal to 1 G.)

At the 8-1/2-minute mark, the main engines cut off. The big external fuel tank, empty now, can be released. As it falls through the atmosphere, the fuel tank will break up into small pieces and burn. About 2 minutes later the commander fires the orbiter's small rear rocket engines to put the spacecraft into orbit. This engine "burn" continues for nearly 2 minutes. The astronauts are lifted off their seats. If it weren't for their seatbelts, they'd float freely in the crew compartment. Their notebooks and pencils bob gently around them. They are now in space!

ROBERT L. CRIPPEN
Born Beaumont, Texas, September 11, 1937

On the morning of April 10, 1981, over 600,000 spectators crowded the beaches and causeways around the Kennedy Space Center to watch the very first launch of the space shuttle. At the controls as *Columbia* blasted off, sending out a wave of heat that people three miles away could feel on their faces, were Commander John Young and Pilot Robert Crippen. Crippen – who later became the most experienced of all shuttle pilots – was going into space for the first time. His heart raced with excitement as he exclaimed, "What a view, what a view!" Meanwhile, John Young's heart was beating at its normal pace. "I was excited too," he joked later. "I just can't make it go any faster."

At Young's right hand was Robert Crippen. Since that first launch, Crippen has become highly respected for his brilliant aviation record – it was, for example, his clever and controlled commanding of *Challenger* in 1984 that ensured the safe retrieval and repair of the Solar Maximum Satellite. As Mission Specialist George Nelson was working outside the orbiter, Crippen suggested he try to stop the rotations of the satellite with his own hands. Even though it was an untested procedure, Nelson gave it a try. It did not work, so Crippen then positioned *Challenger* to within 12 meters of the Solar Max and gently moved around it while Mission Specialist Terry Hart maneuvered the crippled satellite into the orbiter's cargo bay with the robotic arm. This technical feat in space has been compared to steering an elephant around to pick up a penny.

The flight deck of Columbia *on the first flight of the space shuttle. On the left is Commander John Young and on the right is Pilot Robert Crippen.*

Robert H. Goddard of Massachusetts, the American space pioneer, stands beside the first successful liquid-propellant rocket in 1926.

Opposite page: *The eye of* Hurricane Josephine *as seen from the orbiter. This 1984 hurricane measured 500 miles (800 kilometers) across.*

How Do You Become an Astronaut?

To become a Mercury astronaut in 1959, you had to be a man under 40 years of age who held an engineering degree and also be a test pilot with at least 1,500 hours of flying time. (You also had to be shorter than 5 feet 11 inches (178 centimeters) tall to fit into the small Mercury space capsule!)

Today there are more routes to space. Since 1978 the astronaut program has been open to women as well as men. There are now two main kinds of shuttle astronauts: pilot astronauts and mission specialists.

Pilot astronauts actually fly the shuttle. A candidate must:
• have a bachelor's degree in engineering, science, or mathematics;
• have 1,000 hours of flight time as a jet pilot, preferably with test-pilot experience;
• be able to pass a rigorous NASA physical fitness exam for pilots;
• be between 5 feet 4 inches and 6 feet 4 inches (160 and 190 centimeters) tall.

Mission specialists are scientists who do space walks and satellite launches and repairs, and carry out experiments. An applicant must:
• have a bachelor's degree in engineering, science, or mathematics plus an advanced degree or at least three years of related work experience;
• be able to pass a NASA physical fitness exam;
• be between 5 feet and 6 feet 4 inches(150 and 190 centimeters).

NASA (the National Aeronautics and Space Administration, the United States government agency that oversees

the space program) will accept a new group of astronaut candidates in 1990 and every two years after that. Every time NASA invites people to apply to the astronaut program, hundreds of people respond. Only about twenty are chosen. All of them have great academic records and all of them are in excellent health, but they need other qualities, too. NASA looks for people who stay cool in stressful situations, work well with others, and learn new tasks quickly.

Above: Astronauts in training have a brief taste of weightlessness in a KC-135 jet. A series of steep climbs and dives produces 30-second periods of weightlessness.
Above right: Mission Specialist Guion Bluford became the first black astronaut in space on a Challenger *flight in 1983.*

Astronauts are lowered into WET-F (the Weightless Environment Training Facility). The water simulates the weightlessness they will experience in space.

Astronaut candidates need at least two years of classroom work and practical training before they are ready to fly on the shuttle. In their first year they study every part of the shuttle and how it works. They also take classes in engineering, astronomy, geology, and the life sciences. People who are already experts in one area of science have to be willing to start at the beginning in other fields.

The astronaut candidates' practical training is exhausting and sometimes scary. In their survival course they practice parachuting to the ground and into water. They go up in a jet that climbs steeply and then dives to give them a brief taste of weightlessness – about 30 seconds at a time. The astronauts call it the "vomit comet." Pilot astronauts spend hundreds of hours in flight trainers learning how to pilot the orbiter to a safe landing. Mission specialists may practice operating the shuttle's robotic arm, or scientific experiments, or they may find themselves in a bulky space suit at the bottom of a big water tank, practicing for a space walk.

Many astronauts wait six to ten years before they get their first chance to go into space. (The record for the longest wait is 19 years! Don Lind, who became an astronaut in 1966, finally flew on the shuttle in 1985.) In the meantime they carry out all kinds of support tasks. For instance, an astronaut may be a "CapCom" or capsule communicator – usually the only person at Mission Control who communicates directly with the astronauts aboard the shuttle during a mission (although the flight director makes the final decisions about mission operations and many other experts are available to give advice). The CapCom usually trains with the crew before the mission.

There's another way to board the shuttle for people who are not career astronauts. At this time it is also the only way open to non-U.S. citizens, even the ones who are called astronauts in their own countries. This is to be a payload specialist. Payload specialists have a special project to work on in space. Usually they travel on the space shuttle only once, although Charles Walker, who tests medicines in space, has been on three missions.

Payload specialists train with the astronauts of their crew for at least two months before their mission.

Payload Specialist Charles Walker has made three space flights. He tests and develops new medicines in space.

The Wonders of Weightlessness

It's hard not to smile when you see the grins on the astronauts' faces as they float from the flight deck down to the mid deck in *The Dream Is Alive*. Like children trying out a wonderful new game, the astronauts let their food float up so that they can grab it with their mouths. They sleep blissfully with no mattresses or pillows. Weightlessness looks like a lot of fun. What makes it happen?

When we say that something has weight on Earth, we really mean that gravity is pulling it toward the Earth. Gravity is the force that holds you on the Earth and keeps you – and every other Earthly thing – from flying off into space. When you jump up in the air, you quickly come back down. When you let go of a book, it falls to the ground.

Many people think that astronauts are weightless because the shuttle is too far from the Earth to feel the pull of gravity. This isn't so. It is true that the force of gravity gets weaker as you travel away from the Earth. But the

shuttle only goes a few hundred miles up, where gravity is almost as strong as it is on the Earth's surface.

If the Earth's gravity stopped pulling on the shuttle after it left the ground, the shuttle could keep traveling out into space in a straight line. But the pull of gravity continues, and it tugs the shuttle back toward Earth. However, the shuttle is going at the right speed – about 17,000 miles (28,000 kilometers) per hour – so it won't fall straight back to Earth. Instead, the combination of the right speed and the pull of gravity makes the shuttle fall in a curved path that has the same shape as the curve of the Earth. The shuttle goes into orbit around and around the Earth.

At every moment, the orbiting shuttle is falling, but because of its curved path it doesn't get any closer to the Earth. *That's why the astronauts feel weightless.*

Weightlessness makes all kinds

Three well-dressed nineteenth-century gentlemen, a dog, and some chickens experience weightlessness in this fanciful illustration for Jules Verne's novel From the Earth to the Moon *(1865).*

of changes in the astronauts' bodies. Their spines stretch, and they become 1–2 inches (3–5 centimeters) taller. Body fluids shift from the lower parts of their bodies to the upper parts. This causes what the astronauts call "puffy face." Their eyes seem smaller, and they look like chipmunks who have stuffed their cheeks with nuts.

Their voices may sound more nasal, as if they had colds.

The worst effect of weightlessness is space sickness. This is a kind of motion sickness that makes people feel dizzy and may even make them vomit. About half of the astronauts suffer from space sickness, but it's hard to predict who will. People who don't get sick in boats or cars may still get sick in space. Usually space sickness wears off in a couple of days, so NASA doesn't schedule space walks for the early days of a mission.

So that their muscles, including their heart muscles, won't become weak during the time that they're weightless, astronauts have to exercise. The usual Earth exercises won't do – it's too easy to do a one-handed pushup or to lift weights. Instead, the astronauts run on a treadmill that they attach to the floor. They use a belt and a shoulder harness to hold them down so that they can run in place.

Most astronauts say that the hardest thing about weightlessness is saying good-bye to it. They feel heavy and unsteady when they first walk on Earth again. Back at home, one astronaut absentmindedly let go of his cup and was startled when it crashed to the floor instead of floating near his hand!

David Leestma, mission specialist on Mission 41G, floats through Challenger's *mid deck. Notice the lockers on the walls.*

PUTTING IT ALL TOGETHER

Every spacecraft begins its journey at about one mile an hour. This happens a few days before it rockets into space, when it is carried to the launchpad on a slow-moving crawler. The crawler, weighing more than 3,000 tons (2,700 metric tons), is the world's largest land vehicle. It needs a crew of thirteen people, including three drivers, for the four-mile trip from the Vehicle Assembly Building at the Kennedy Space Center to the launchpad.

This vast building – which stands 525 feet (160 meters) tall, covers 8 acres (3 hectares) of land, and can be seen from many miles away – was once used to assemble the huge Saturn moon rockets. Today it is where all the main pieces of the shuttle are put together: two solid rocket boosters (SRBs), an external fuel tank, and the orbiter.

The SRBs – 149 feet (45 meters) long and 12 feet (3.5 meters) across – are the largest solid rockets ever flown, and the first ever designed to be reused. (For more on rockets, see p. 12.) One rocket booster is attached to each side of the external fuel tank. The SRBs are made in sections. Each section is filled with solid fuel, leaving a hollow core through the middle. Then all the sections are stacked and sealed.

At lift-off, both rockets are ignited from the top. The flame runs right down the hollow middle, burning from the center out to the walls of the rocket. All the fuel is used up in the first two minutes of flight. The empty rocket cases parachute down from the shuttle and are fished out of the ocean. Soon they're back at the Kennedy Space Center, after having been cleaned and filled for the next shuttle flight.

The external fuel tank is the largest part of the shuttle. It has the same shape as the feed silos you see on farms, but it is much bigger: 154 feet (47 meters) tall and more than 27 feet (8 meters) across. It is attached to the belly of the orbiter and feeds liquid fuel into the orbiter's three main engines.

On the first two shuttle missions the fuel tanks had a top coat of white paint, but now they're launched in their orange undercoats. The tank doesn't look as bright and shiny, but just leaving off one coat of paint makes it 600 pounds (275 kilograms) lighter!

The external tank pours all its fuel into the orbiter engines in the first 8-1/2 minutes of flight. Then it, too, falls away, breaking up and burning as it reenters Earth's atmosphere.

By the time the shuttle reaches orbit around the Earth, it has burned up thousands of tons of fuel and dropped hundreds of tons of SRBs and tank. All that remains is the orbiter, about the size of a DC-9 air-

***Below**: The orbiter as it looks in space. The cargo bay doors are open throughout the mission to keep the orbiter from heating up too much. Note the remote manipulator system (robotic arm) lifted out of the bay.*

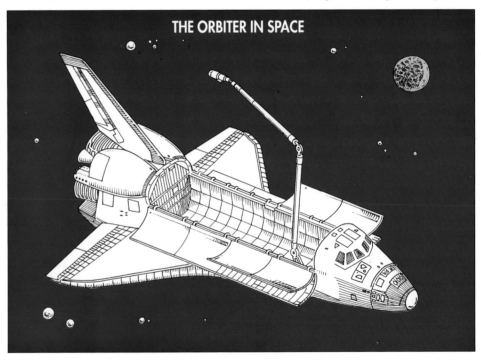

THE ORBITER IN SPACE

***Opposite page**: Thousands of people work behind the scenes to keep the shuttles flying. In this picture, two satellites that were brought back to Earth for repairs are being unloaded from the cargo bay of the orbiter.*

Opposite page: Workers install heat shield tiles on the orbiter. The tiles range in thickness from 0.5 inches (1.27 centimeters) to 5 inches (12.7 centimeters), depending on where they are placed. No two are exactly the same.

plane. The orbiter, unlike any other American spacecraft, can be used over and over because its 78-foot (24-meter) wingspan allows it to glide back to Earth for an airplanelike landing. The orbiter's aluminum framework is covered with special protective materials so that it can survive temperatures up to 3000° F (1650° C) as it reenters Earth's atmosphere.

The orbiter has three kinds of engines. The three powerful main engines are at the rear of the orbiter. These engines and the solid rocket boosters get the shuttle off the ground. The main engines cut out when the fuel tank drops away, and they're not used again on the mission.

Two smaller rear engines, called the Orbital Maneuvering System (OMS), are fired to put the orbiter into orbit. They're fired again at the end of the mission to get the orbiter out of orbit so it can fly home. The Reaction Control System (RCS) has 44 small rocket engines that can move the orbiter up and down and from side to side while it is in space.

The shuttle's job is to transport astronauts into space where they can place satellites in orbit, retrieve and repair orbiting spacecraft, conduct scientific experiments, and perform other necessary tasks. The cargo bay (also called the payload bay) is the biggest part of the orbiter. Its area of 60 by 15 feet (18.3 by 4.6 meters) is big enough for five African elephants or a large tour bus, although no one has yet asked to send any of these things into space! Instead, the cargo bay usually contains satellites or science experiments.

In *The Dream Is Alive* you get an astronaut's-eye view of the cargo bay from the aft (rear) windows of the crew cabin. This is where James van Hoften and George Nelson repaired the Solar Max satellite and where Kathryn Sullivan and David Leestma took a space walk. Along one side of the cargo bay the Canadian-made Remote Manipulator System (also called the robotic arm or Canadarm) is held by a set of brackets until it's needed.

On some shuttle missions the cargo bay contains Spacelab, which was designed and built by the European Space Agency. The enclosed laboratory is about 9 feet (2.7 meters) long and 13 feet (4 meters) across, but sometimes two lab sections are joined together to make a longer work area. The lab is connected to the crew cabin by a round passageway. Like the cabin,

THE INCREDIBLE TILES

They sound like science fiction, but they're real: You can hold them in your bare hands while they're still glowing white-hot, because their surface can cool down so fast. They are as light as balsa wood, yet strong enough to protect a spaceship hurtling through the atmosphere. Over 20,000 of these amazing tiles cover parts of each orbiter. And their main ingredient is something we're all familiar with – sand!

To make these tiles, the sand is finely crushed and stiffened with clay. Each tile is cut to fit a particular place on the orbiter, and no two are exactly the same. They're covered with a shiny glass black or white coating. Black tiles are glued to the parts of the orbiter that heat up to 1200°–2300° F (650°–1260° C) during reentry, such as the undersides of its wings. (At these temperatures the unprotected aluminum frame of the orbiter wouldn't just melt into liquid, it would boil!) White tiles go on areas of the orbiter that stay slightly cooler (700°–1200° F, or 370°–650° C), such as the sides of the crew compartment.

Amazing as the tiles are, they have drawbacks. It took thousands of hours to install them in their proper places on the first orbiter, *Columbia*. And it turned out that some tiles were usually knocked off during each launch and reentry. Although the loss of these tiles was never enough to endanger a mission, they had to be replaced before the orbiter could fly again. Later orbiters have a few thousand less tiles than *Columbia* did. Instead, some areas are covered with quilted silica (glass) fiber material that is easier to install and repair.

the lab has temperature controls and air to breathe, so scientists can work there in normal clothes. Every surface is covered with computers, workbenches, instrument racks, and other scientific equipment. On some missions there may even be cages of monkeys and rats. Outside the enclosed lab there are open "pallets," which are racks of experiments exposed to space.

The orbiter crew cabin has three levels. The "top" level (top and bottom don't mean much in space) is the flight deck. The forward area – with its wide windows, hundreds of dials and switches, and video displays – looks a lot like the cockpit of a passenger jet. The commander and the pilot sit here and use

These mung bean seedlings were sprouted on the shuttle as part of a science experiment on plant growth in space.

these controls when the shuttle is being launched, whenever they're making a change in the orbiter's flight path, and when they bring the orbiter back to Earth.

The aft area of the flight deck is the mission work station, with computer keyboards, closed-circuit TV screens, and controls for the robot arm. The work station has windows that face back toward the cargo bay and more windows in the ceiling. Whenever the orbiter flies "upside down" during the mission, these ceiling windows give the astronauts their best view of Earth. When you see the astronauts stretching "up"

BUMBLING BEES AND SPIDERS IN A SPIN

Mission Specialist James van Hoften watches the honey bee colony as they find out how to fly in space.

While the crew of Mission 41C were getting used to weightlessness, their 3,300 passengers were figuring it out too. The passengers were a box full of honeybees, complete with their queen. They were part of a student experiment to see how they would adjust to spaceflight. Astronaut James van Hoften noticed that the bees took about as long as he did to learn how to move. "They couldn't figure out that flight didn't work. They'd just beat their wings and go the wrong way. They finally learned, as we did, to push off and just drift." The honeybees not only learned how to use their wings in space, they made 30 square inches (190 square centimeters) of honeycomb during the 6-day mission. This is about what they would have made on the ground. The first few comb cells had an odd shape, but the rest looked like the ones bees make on Earth. When the orbiter first returned to Earth's gravity, the bees fell in a heap at the bottom of their box. But one day later they were back to normal, visiting flowers and gathering pollen.

Although these were the first bees to work in space, some distant cousins of theirs went first. Two spiders named Arabella and Anita were taken aboard Skylab, the U.S. orbiting space station, in 1973. Scientists guessed they wouldn't be able to spin webs in space. After all, think how hard it would be to work those sticky strands into the right pattern when they were all floating in midair instead of hanging down. But Arabella and Anita surprised the experts, making webs that were almost as good as the ones they could spin on Earth.

Opposite page: The forward flight deck of Discovery, *with over 2,020 separate displays and controls. Commander Henry Hartsfield (left) and Pilot Michael Coats (right) plan how to position the orbiter so that mission specialists can release a satellite into proper orbit.*

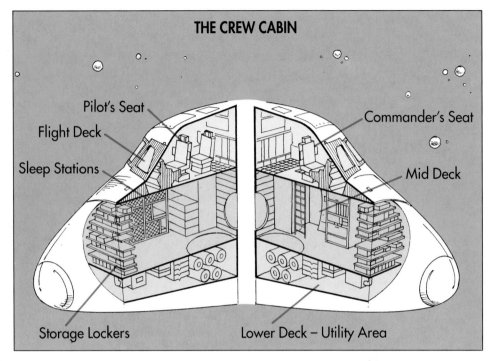

THE CREW CABIN

Pilot's Seat

Flight Deck

Sleep Stations

Storage Lockers

Commander's Seat

Mid Deck

Lower Deck – Utility Area

to look out these windows in *The Dream Is Alive*, it's hard to remember that they're looking not toward space, but toward home!

Below the flight deck is the mid deck, which is only about 10 feet (3 meters) long and about 11 feet (3.3 meters) wide. But this small space is kitchen, bedroom, bathroom, office – and even gymnasium and laboratory – for all the astronauts. Every inch of the mid deck is put to use. There's a small galley kitchen where the astronauts take turns preparing meals, and there's a sink and a toilet. There are four bunks – or "sleep stations," as NASA calls them. The walls are covered with small storage lockers containing the astronauts' spare clothes, the few personal belongings they're allowed to bring, tools for their experiments, medical supplies, and so on. Each locker is labeled to show what's inside. The hatch the astronauts use to board the shuttle and the airlock that leads outside for astronauts doing space walks are both in the mid deck.

Under the floor of the mid deck is the utility area. Here there is space to stow garbage. It is also full of wires and cables for the orbiter's life support systems which provide air to breathe, light, and warmth inside the orbiter. Outside, as the astronauts can never quite forget, is the vast, cold blackness of space.

Opposite page: In the orbiter's airlock Kathryn Sullivan is helped into the top half of the space suit she will wear for her first space walk. You can see the metal ring joints that join the top and bottom halves of the suit, and the ones that join the sleeves to the gloves.

FROM SPACE TO YOU

Many of the things we use every day owe something to the space program. Sometimes it's easy to see the connection. Freeze-dried foods for fast meals at home are pretty close to the meals the astronauts eat. But sometimes it's a surprise to find out that a product has anything to do with space research. Did you know that many athletic shoes have a layer of cushioning in the soles that was first developed for walking on the moon? The space program has also improved your eyeglasses and sunglasses: Plastic lenses are lighter on your nose than glass lenses, and they won't shatter if they're hit. But until recently they could get scratched very easily. Now many lenses are covered with a tough, clear coating that was first developed to protect plastic equipment in space.

These sports shoes are made of materials that were first used in astronauts' moon-walk boots.

HELLO, LDEF

On the morning of January 12, 1990, groups of scientists in the United States, Canada, and Western Europe held their breath. They had waited 5-1/2 years for this moment. Would the space shuttle be able to rescue the satellite that held their experiments? As they watched on television, Commander Dan Brandenstein brought the orbiter close to the huge satellite so that Mission Specialist Bonnie Dunbar could use the wire "hand" of the robotic arm to snare it. LDEF, battered by space debris and burned by the sun, was finally coming back to Earth.

LDEF (pronounced el-def) stands for the Long Duration Exposure Facility. This shiny 12-sided satellite, as big as a school bus, was deployed during Mission 41C in 1984. LDEF was supposed to be picked up by the shuttle after one year. But first the shuttle schedule fell behind, and then the *Challenger* accident shut down the shuttle program for 2-1/2 years. By the time LDEF was recaptured, it was only weeks away from falling out of orbit and burning up.

Above: LDEF, after it was deployed by Mission 41C in 1984.

Opposite page: This is the view the astronauts see from the aft windows of the flight deck. The cargo bay is at the bottom of the picture, and LDEF, which weighs 21,400 pounds (9,700 kilograms) on Earth, is about to float gently away from the orbiter.

LDEF was covered with trays of different materials to see what would happen to them if they were left in space for a long time. Some trays contained paints and building materials that might someday be used for the space station. Could they stand up to the extreme temperatures of space, to cosmic rays and tiny pelting meteorites? Other trays tested the effects of space on living things such as shrimp eggs. And then there were the tomato seeds – 12.5 million of them. These seeds have been sent to science classrooms all over North America so that students from fifth grade right through college will be able to find out for themselves whether space changes the way plants grow.

The Shuttle's Extra Hand

The Remote Manipulator System has lifted the Solar Max satellite out of the orbiter's cargo bay and is ready to release it.

Although most of the space shuttle's components are built in the United States, the Remote Manipulator System (also known as the robotic arm or Canadarm) was designed and built in Canada.

The arm, made of lightweight tubing, is just over 50 feet (15 meters) long, and jointed at the "shoulder," "elbow," and "wrist."

The arm also has a hand, although it doesn't look much like a human hand. It's a ring of metal holding three pieces of strong wire that can be pulled tight around a jutting piece on a satellite called the grapple fixture.

The joints are driven by small motors, and the arm also has its own built-in heaters to keep it at the right temperature in space. The joystick controls for the arm are in the aft area of the flight deck. Astronauts can keep an eye on how the arm is moving by looking out the rear windows, which give a clear view of the cargo bay. Since the arm has two television cameras, mounted on its wrist and elbow, the astronauts can also check the arm's movements on TV monitors.

The arm's main job is to move satellites around. It can lift them out of the cargo bay as gently as a mother cat picking up her kittens and launch them into space. It can also pluck satellites out of orbit and lower them into the cargo bay. Then they can be repaired during a space walk or brought back to earth. One of the largest satellites the arm has deployed and recaptured is LDEF (see p. 28), which weighs 15,000 pounds (6,800 kilograms) on Earth.

The arm has other tricks up its padded, white-painted sleeve. Sometimes it's used as a "cherry picker" to lift astronauts up so they can retrieve orbiting satellites. (These are usually older satellites that were made without grapple fixtures for the arm to grab.) The astronauts float off the end of the arm, anchored only by clamps holding their feet. Once the satellites are in the cargo bay, the arm makes a handy work platform for astronauts carrying out repairs.

Mission 51D in 1985 was faced with a satellite that had a power failure after it was launched. Mission control decided that it was too risky for astronauts to approach the satellite, because it might suddenly switch itself on and injure them. Instead the crew made a "flyswatter" tool of things they had on board – including two plastic notebook covers. Then two space-walking astronauts attached the tool to the end of the arm so that Mission Specialist Rhea Seddon could use it to hook the power switch on the side of the satellite.

Unfortunately, this ingenious rescue attempt was not successful.

Perhaps the arm's finest achievement to date came on the Solar Max repair mission (41C). Astronauts James van Hoften and George Nelson had spent long months before the mission practicing the recapture of this satellite. But when Nelson tried to grab the satellite with a special tool he had been given for the job, he found that it did not fit!

Solar Max, a $235-million satellite designed to study the sun, was tumbling uselessly in space. It looked as if the mission was a failure. Then Commander Robert Crippen, with the last of his maneuvering fuel, brought the orbiter up close to the satellite, and Mission Specialist Terry Hart grabbed it with the robotic arm. The astronauts and the people at Mission Control were overjoyed.

Opposite page: With his work on Solar Max completed, astronaut James van Hoften takes the MMU (manned maneuvering unit) for a test drive in the orbiter's cargo bay. The Canadian-made robotic arm is on the right side of the picture.

Filming in Space

When you watch an IMAX film such as *The Dream Is Alive*, you'll probably be too busy watching the sweeping panoramas to wonder how the film was made. But later on, you may well be curious. What makes the large-format IMAX film look different from an ordinary film? Who filmed the scenes that you see in *The Dream Is Alive*? What kind of equipment did they use?

Most films you see in theaters are shot on 35 millimeter film (film measuring 35 millimeters in width). IMAX films are shot on 65 millimeter film stock with film frames that are 10 times the size of a normal film. This gives a sharper picture. These pictures are projected onto a huge screen, up to eight stories high, with a projector that uses a special Rolling Loop system which holds each frame steadier and lights it more brightly than an ordinary projector. A powerful sound system adds to the sensation of being in the picture.

There's no room on the space shuttle for filmmakers. So the only way to get a film made in space is to teach the astronauts how to do it themselves. The teachers were producer and director Graeme Ferguson and cinematographer (a person who films with the camera) David Douglas, who spent a year teaching 14 astronauts how to use the IMAX camera and equipment.

During a training session, Sally Ride takes a look through the viewfinder of an IMAX camera.

Each astronaut received about 25 hours of training.

The film production team talked to the astronauts and looked at the mission plans for the three flights that would have the IMAX camera on board. Then they made up a "wish list" of things they hoped the astronauts would film. Each roll of IMAX film runs three minutes, and each shuttle mission could carry only a limited number of rolls. So it was important to plan carefully. Once the shuttle was launched, Graeme Ferguson and his team worked in shifts, to be available 24 hours a day to answer the astronauts' questions about filming.

The IMAX camera, which weighs about 80 pounds (about 36 kilograms) on Earth, weighs nothing at all in space. At first the camera presented some surprises for the astronauts and for the filmmakers on the ground, but these were soon resolved. For example, the film stock, which was tightly rolled on cores, loosened in space. The astronauts had to be careful not to let the film fall off the center core when they were loading it

into the camera. All of the pictures taken from space in this book were shot by astronauts, so you can see for yourself how well they did. Some crew members said that the IMAX camera was like having another person along. They called it "Max." Some of the best scenes in *The Dream Is Alive* were the astronauts' own ideas: the crew sleeping with their arms floating up in front of their bodies; two astronauts smiling and peeking back through the windows from outside the orbiter.

The Dream Is Alive also features thundering blastoffs filmed by IMAX cinematographers. In one case a remote camera (one that can be operated from a distance) was placed right on the launch tower, inside a fireproof box . As astronaut David Leestma joked about the very real wonders shown in the film, "The special effects are pretty good."

Right: *Terry Hart shows how to balance a heavy IMAX film magazine on one finger in zero gravity.*

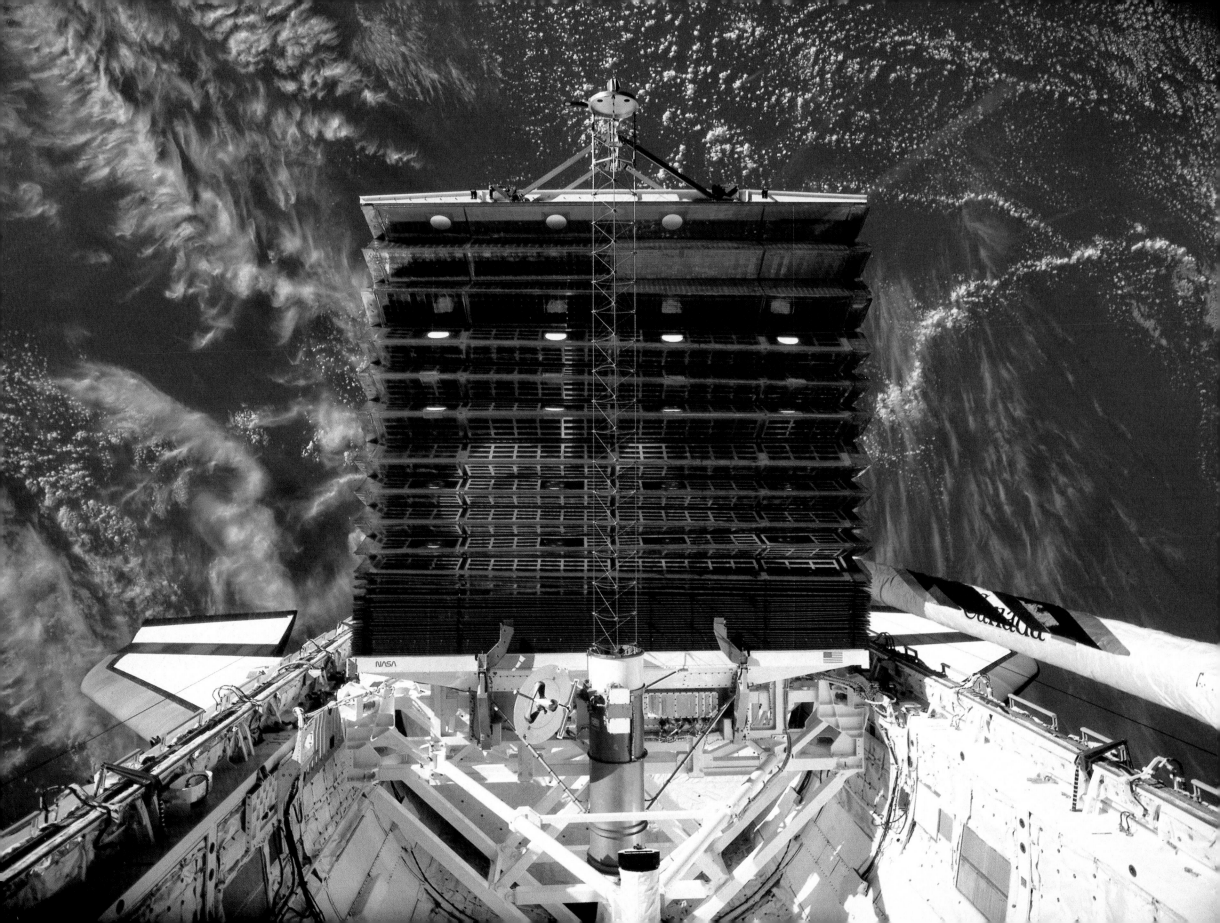

A DAY IN SPACE

It's morning on the orbiter. Sunrise comes every 90 minutes in orbit, but the astronauts keep to the same schedule as Mission Control in Houston. It's time to get up when the ground flight controllers wake them. Mission Control tries to start astronauts off on their workday in good humor. For instance, the morning after a 1990 shuttle mission recaptured the LDEF satellite, Mission Control serenaded the astronauts to the tune of "Hello Dolly": "Well hello LDEF, it's so nice to have you back where you belong." One morning on Mission 41G, Sally Ride had her own joke ready for Mission Control: "We're not in right now. If you leave your name and number, we'll get back to you."

The whole crew – usually five to seven people – has just 45 minutes to get washed and dressed. Anyone who wants privacy can pull a curtain across the sink and toilet area. There's also a light and a mirror in this "bathroom," and strips of tape hold each astronaut's washcloth and towel to the wall. There's no shower aboard the orbiter. Instead, the astronauts use their washcloths to give themselves sponge baths. The sink has a clear plastic cover over it to keep the water from flying out. The cover has two hand-size openings in it so the astronauts can reach in to wash their hands or wet their washcloths.

Someone makes breakfast (all the astronauts take turns making meals) while the others get started on their day's work. It costs well over $100 million to launch the shuttle for each mission, so the astronauts

are expected to keep busy. They work at least 12 hours a day, and almost every minute is scheduled in advance.

Launching satellites for the U.S. government (or, in the past, private companies) has been an important part of the work on most shuttle flights. Mission 41D, for instance, launched three communications satellites. It takes teamwork to launch a satellite. The commander or pilot maneuvers the orbiter into just the right position, and then several mission specialists work together to release the satellite from the cargo bay and check its position through the flight-deck windows. Some satellites are launched by the robotic arm, operated by a mission specialist who has spent months learning how to control it.

Mission specialists and payload specialists also spend time doing experiments. For instance, on

Above: *The progress of manned space flight from the early Mercury missions into the future.*

Opposite page: *Mission Specialist Judith Resnik unfolded this solar array panel from inside the orbiter on Mission 41D. The leaves are so thin that the 105-foot-tall structure can fold into a box just 7 inches (18 centimeters) high.*

Mission 41G Payload Specialist Marc Garneau carried out 10 science experiments, including one to find out whether people's sense of taste changes in space. Astronauts often complain that their food tastes bland. Since a big part of the sense of taste is really the sense of smell, scientists are trying to find out whether food tastes funny in space because weightlessness makes people's faces swell and blocks their noses. On Mission 41D, Payload Specialist Charles

Walker worked on developing new medicines that can be made in better, purer form in the weightlessness of space.

Some of the work on the orbiter is just housekeeping, but it has to be done. Crumbs are vacuumed up before they can float into the orbiter's electrical systems. Germs can spread very quickly in the small crew cabin, so the kitchen and bathroom areas are cleaned with germ-killing wipes. Dirty clothing and used food containers are put in sealed plastic bags and stowed under the mid deck. Because there's so little room, everything has to be put away right after it's used. Besides, you can't simply set a fork down with the idea of putting it away later. It will just float away!

On the first few days of a mission, the astronauts are still trying to get used to their own weightlessness. The astronauts who have been in space before know just how hard to push off from a wall to get where they want to go. The newcomers push off too hard and end up crashing into the far wall. Or they push off too lightly, and end up stranded in the middle of the cabin, making useless swimming motions.

The astronauts' favorite leisure activity, if they have any free time, is looking out the windows. Earth doesn't look like the blue globe the Apollo astronauts saw from the moon. Because the orbiter is only a

HOW TO GO TO THE BATHROOM IN SPACE

When astronauts visit schools, there's one important question they are always asked: How do you go to the bathroom in space? On the shuttle there is a toilet, but it's not quite the same as the one in your home. First of all, it's not easy to sit on a toilet seat when you're weightless. The space toilet solves this problem. When you sit down, you put a seat belt around your waist and slide your feet into two clips. There are also handholds you can use to keep yourself in place. Because there's no gravity to pull waste down into the toilet, you flip a switch that turns on an air-suction system. Wastes are pulled down into a tank, where they're shredded, dried, and disinfected.

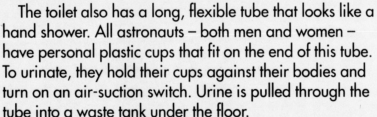

The toilet also has a long, flexible tube that looks like a hand shower. All astronauts – both men and women – have personal plastic cups that fit on the end of this tube. To urinate, they hold their cups against their bodies and turn on an air-suction switch. Urine is pulled through the tube into a waste tank under the floor.

While out on an extravehicular activity, or EVA (space walk), astronauts wear bulky space suits. What happens if they need a toilet while outside the orbiter? The same thing that happens to a small child bundled up in a snowsuit: Either they hold on until they're back inside, or they go in their suits. The astronauts are wearing special underwear, so that in case of a sudden urge to go, the suit will stay dry.

Opposite page: Earth exercises aren't effective in space – it's too easy to do a one-handed pushup when you're weightless! Instead, the astronauts run on a treadmill attached to the floor or a wall. Mission Specialist Steve Hawley has a belt and shoulder harness to hold him down so that he can run in place on the treadmill.

couple of hundred miles up, the astronauts can see details of mountains and rivers. They can see all the different blues of the world's oceans. They can even make out the vapor trails of airplanes, the wakes of ships, and smoke from forest fires. They can see lightning flashing in Earth's thunderstorms.

The astronauts are allowed three one-hour breaks for meals. Mission Control tries not to interrupt them at this time, because it's a rare chance for them to relax and chat together.

The crew cabin of the orbiter is a very small living area by Earth standards. How can six, seven – sometimes even eight – people possibly live and work together for a week in such crowded conditions?

Part of the answer goes right back to the time these people were chosen as astronauts. NASA isn't just looking for great pilots and talented scientists, doctors, and engineers. They're looking for people who can work well with others, and who won't get upset when things go wrong. Although there have never been any orbiter emergencies in space, almost every mission has its annoying problems. On Mission 41G, with seven people aboard, the cooling system broke down. The temperature soared to 95° F (35° C), but the astronauts kept doing their work without complaining. Commander Robert Crippen joked that it was no worse than "late August in Houston."

Before going on a shuttle mission, the crew trains together for a long time – sometimes a year or more. Even the payload specialists, who are not regular astronauts, work with their mission crew for about two months. Each person rehearses over and over the special tasks he or she will have. For instance, James van Hoften and George Nelson of Mission 41C practiced satellite repairs in a water tank (which is the closest they can get to weightlessness on Earth). But the astronauts also practice working together, and they get to know each other very well.

The commander and pilot spend hours in the shuttle simulator, a computer-driven version of the orbiter's flight deck. They can see computer-generated images of the mission through the windows. When they work the controls, the simulator moves as the orbiter would on a real flight. The astronauts also practice in the orbiter trainer, which looks just like the flight deck and mid deck. Just before the flight, the crew works through several days of the mission step by step, going home only to sleep. So by the time they get into space, the cramped crew cabin is a very familiar place.

In fact, the orbiter seems roomier in space than it does on Earth. Once the launch seats are folded away (only the commander's and pilot's seats stay), there is no furniture taking up room. And since the astronauts don't have to stand on the floor, they can use the whole crew cabin. For example, on one mission Steven Hawley exercised on the mid-deck floor while Charles Walker did a science experiment on the wall.

Finally the long work day comes to an end and it's time to get some sleep. The astronauts are allowed

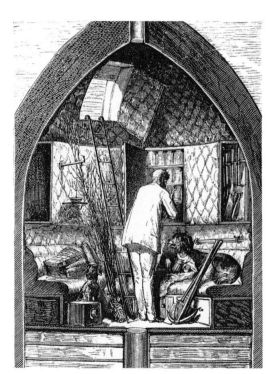

This is the imaginary crew cabin drawn by the illustrator of Jules Verne's From the Earth to the Moon *in 1865.*

Opposite page: *An astronaut practices for the Solar Max rescue and repair mission in the water tank at the Johnson Space Center in Houston. On a space walk, astronauts can move around by themselves in their bulky space suits, but in the water they have to be moved around by helpers in diving gear.*

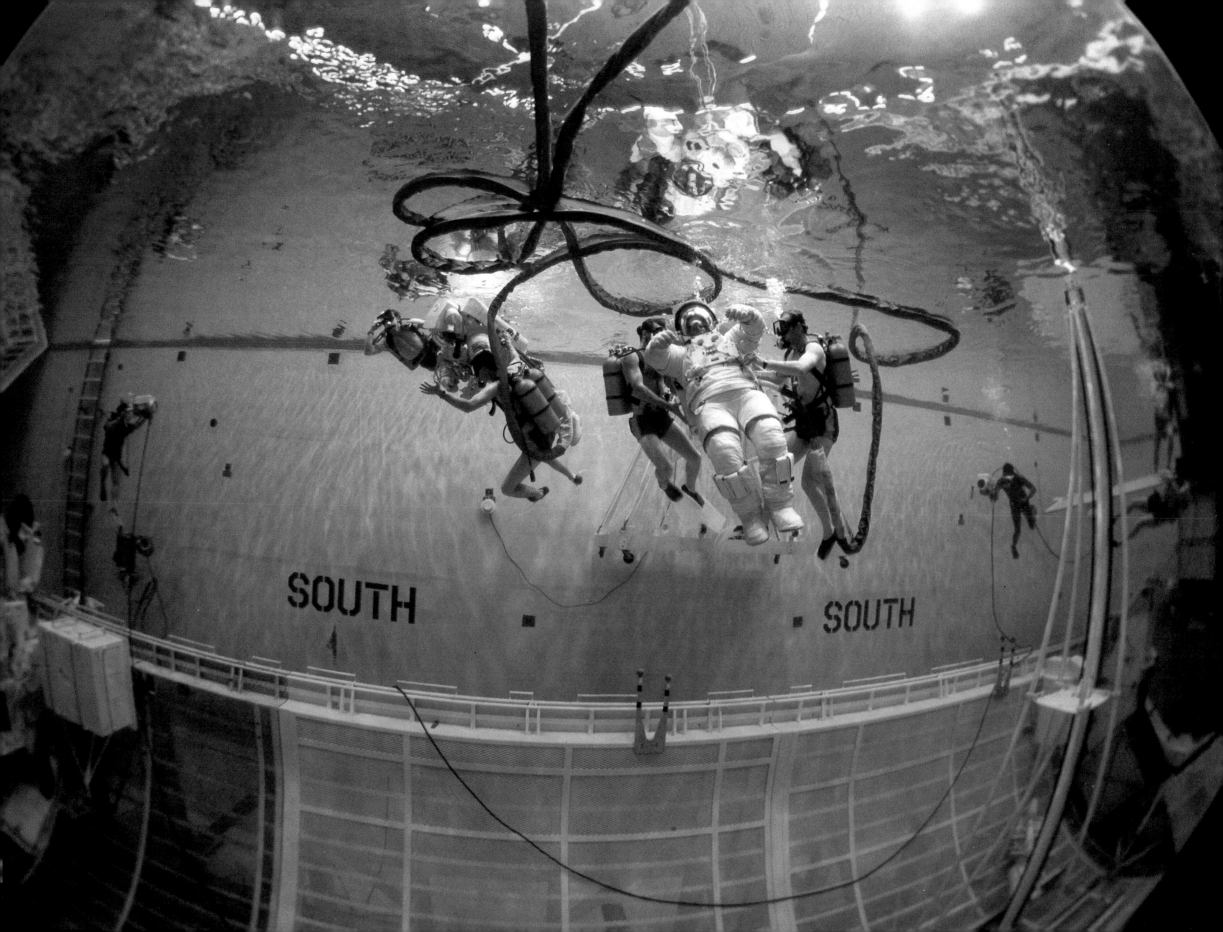

eight hours of rest, although most of them find that they don't need more than six. On most shuttle missions everyone goes to sleep at the same time. (On Spacelab missions the crews usually sleep and work in shifts so that they can get as many experiments done as possible.)

MARC GARNEAU
Born Quebec City, Quebec, Canada, February 23, 1949

When the National Research Council of Canada announced that it was setting up a Canadian astronaut program in 1983, some 4,400 people applied. Marc Garneau, a commander in the Canadian armed forces, was one of five men and one woman who were chosen – and the first one assigned to go into space.

Garneau was the second non-U.S. citizen to be a payload specialist on the shuttle. During 8 days in space on Mission 41G in 1984, he carried out 65 hours of experiments. Some of his experiments had to do with the effects of weightlessness, including space sickness. Garneau had had trouble with motion sickness all through his naval career, and he expected to be sick in space. However, to his surprise, he felt fine, even when he tried to make himself sick for the sake of science!

The 41G crew of seven was the largest group the shuttle had carried up to that time. But Garneau said the close quarters didn't bother him. As a hobby, he had twice sailed across the Atlantic Ocean in a 59-foot (18-meter) yawl with twelve other crew members.

Near the end of the mission the astronauts had a phone call from President Reagan, who joked: "With all there is to do on this mission, I know that Crip (Commander Crippen) appreciates having three strong Canadian arms." Two belonged to Marc Garneau, and the third was the Canadian-designed robotic arm!

On some missions there are four "sleep stations" that look like bunk beds. Three of them are horizontal on a wall of the mid deck, and one of them is vertical. Each one has a light, a storage area, and an air duct. The astronauts sleep inside sleeping bags attached to padded boards. They don't need a soft mattress underneath them when they're weightless, but the feeling of being anchored to something is comforting.

On other missions the astronauts sleep in zippered cotton sleeping bags that attach to the wall. Sally Ride liked to take her sleeping bag up to the flight deck and go to sleep there listening to tapes of her favorite music. Some crew members don't even bother with sleeping bags. Marc Garneau just nodded off in a corner. Sometimes other crew members would find him, sound asleep, drifting through the cabin.

All the astronauts have sleep masks to help them blot out the lights of the orbiter. (They also shield the astronauts from the light that floods through the orbiter windows every time the sun "rises." This happens five times during an 8-hour sleep period.) Soon everyone's fast asleep, high above the Earth. The on-board computers and the flight controllers on the ground watch over the orbiter until morning arrives again.

Opposite page: The Mission 41D crew, asleep in space. Because they're weightless, astronauts can be just as comfortable in a sleeping bag attached to the wall as they are "lying down."

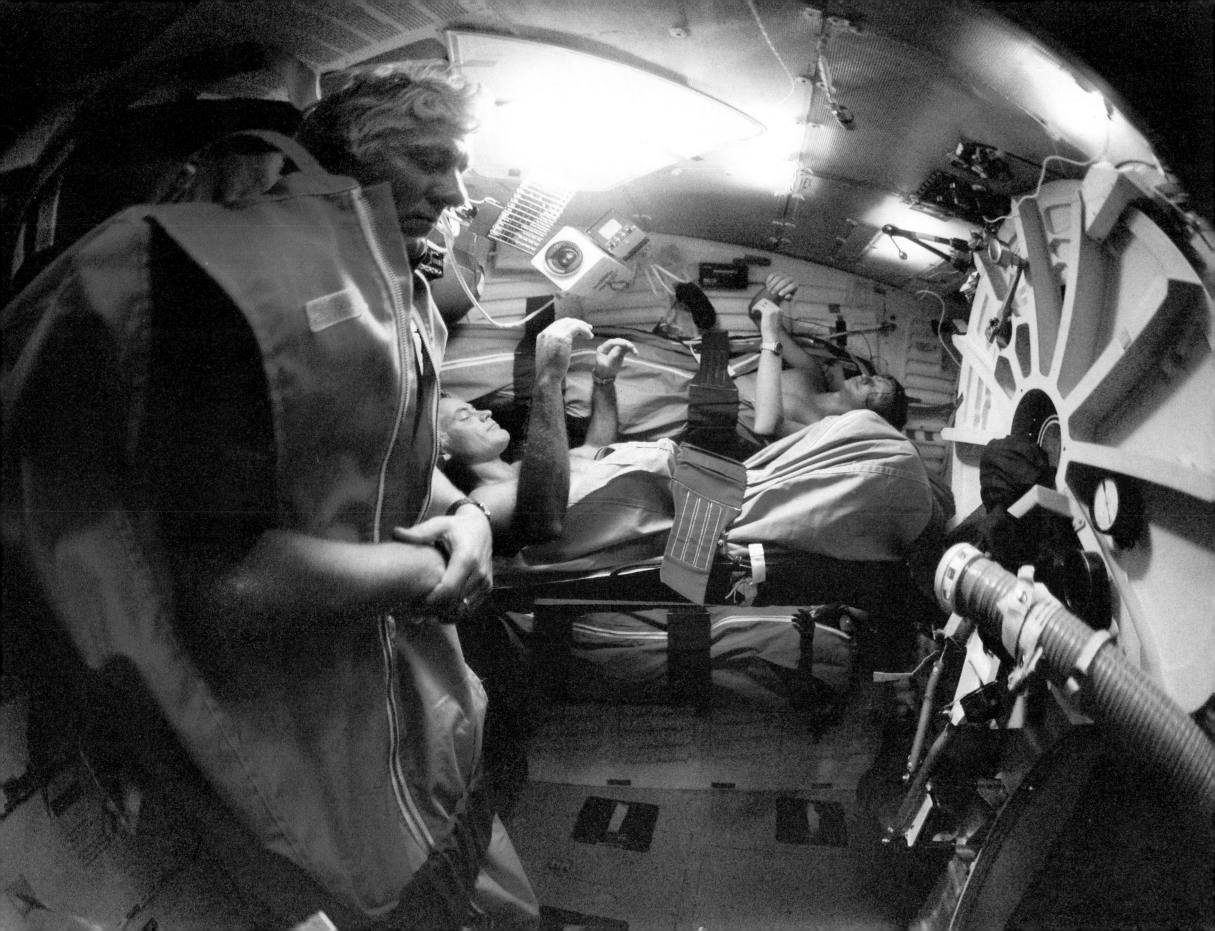

DANGEROUS SPACE DEBRIS

Above: *After five years in space, scientists found that the surface of LDEF was greatly pitted by dust-sized micrometeoroids.*

People have been putting satellites into orbit for more than 30 years. Space debris is the little bits and pieces they leave behind – satellites and satellite parts that are worn out; pieces from exploded rockets; nuts and bolts; even a camera lens accidentally dropped by an astronaut during a space walk. There's more of this debris every year. On each mission the shuttle faces a 1-in-30 chance of hitting debris already circling the earth. NASA thinks this could rise to a 1-in-10 chance by the year 2000. Because it's traveling so fast, a piece of garbage only 3 or 4 inches (8 centimeters) long could hit the shuttle with the force of an explosion. Even bits too small to be seen can do damage. The shuttle has glass windows more than 2 inches thick, made of three layers of glass. Yet when a tiny speck of paint hit *Challenger* in 1983, the window was pitted so deeply that the whole pane had to be replaced.

No one has come up with a good way to clean up this junk. Engineers say that an orbiting "vacuum cleaner" satellite would be too expensive to operate. Instead, NASA is working on protective shields and warning systems to protect the shuttle from debris. They are also trying to find ways to cut down on new space garbage.

Right: *The Syncom IV (Leasat-2) satellite departs from* Discovery's *cargo bay in a frisbee-like manner.*

Opposite page: *Kathryn Sullivan and David Leestma, all ready to leave the orbiter for a walk in space.*

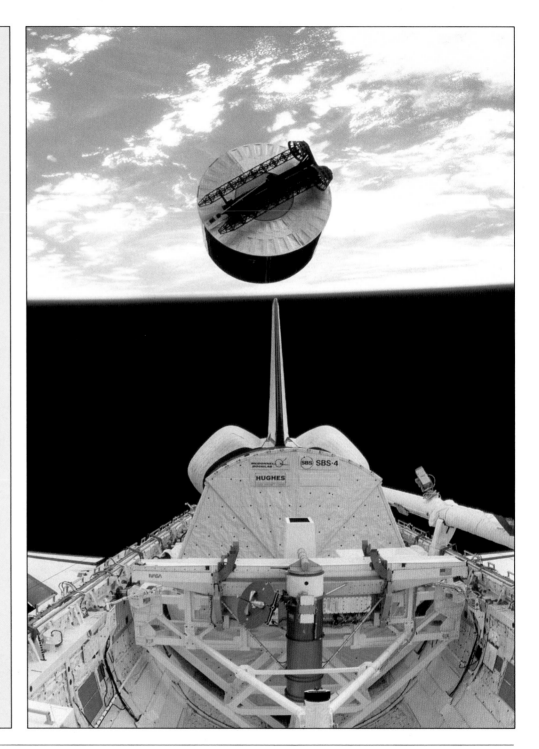

Space Food

On his first spaceflight in 1965, Gemini astronaut John Young smuggled a corned beef sandwich aboard. The people at Mission Control were aghast. They worried that floating crumbs might damage electrical circuits in the spacecraft. Still, they understood why Young brought the sandwich. Official space food in those days wasn't very tasty.

John Glenn, the first American to orbit the earth in 1962, used squeeze tubes that looked like toothpaste tubes, filled with pureed food that was like baby food. Later astronauts ate bite-sized cubes of meat, fruit, bread, and dessert, all coated with gelatin so they wouldn't crumble.

By the time John Young commanded the space-lab shuttle mission in 1983, he had no need for a smuggled sandwich. Finally, astronauts could dine on turkey tetrazzini or shrimp creole. They could drink fruit drinks, tea, coffee, or cocoa, and snack on puddings, cookies, and fruit.

The orbiter galley is only about the size of a large drink vending machine, but it has a lot packed into it. The galley has hot and cold water, a small oven, serving trays, wet and dry wipes for cleaning up, and cutlery. Storage compartments contain almost 100 different kinds of foods and 20 kinds of drinks. The astronauts eat three meals a day, and on a 6-day mission they never have to eat the same meal twice.

Here's what one astronaut ate in a day on a recent shuttle mission:

Dinnertime on the mid deck of Discovery, *with the crew of Mission 41D. Mission Specialist Mike Mullane, in the middle, is spinning a shrimp.*

Breakfast:	Diced peaches
	Scrambled eggs
	Bran flakes
	Cocoa
	Orange-grapefruit drink
Lunch:	Chicken salad spread
	Bread
	Fruit cocktail
	Almonds
	Lemonade
Dinner:	Chicken teriyaki
	Potato patty
	Creamed spinach
	Candy-coated peanuts
	Vanilla pudding
	Tea

All space food is prepared before the flight. It has to be food that bacteria cannot spoil, because there is no refrigerator on the shuttle. The food must weigh as little as possible and take up as little space as possible. And the food must be fast and easy to fix, because there's no chef on board – the crew members take turns preparing meals.

The lightest, easiest way to take food into space is in dried form. Food won't spoil in this state, either. In the menu above, the scrambled eggs, chicken teriyaki, and dinner vegetables were pack-

aged this way. Thermostabilized food is cooked on Earth and sealed in cans. This is how the chicken salad spread, the fruit cocktail, and the vanilla pudding were prepared. A few desserts and snacks, such as the almonds and candy-coated peanuts, are eaten in exactly the same form as on Earth.

It takes the food server only about 30 minutes to fix meals for everybody. The food is already divided into individual servings,

A tray of orbiter food, ready to eat.

inside a pouch marked with the day and the meal. The server just has to find the right pouch and take out all the food. A hollow needle is used to poke a hole in the plastic dried-food containers and add water to them. Anything that needs to be heated is popped in the oven. When all the little food containers are fitted into each person's food tray, it's time to eat.

What's it like to eat a meal when you're weightless? Well, first of all, you don't have to sit at a table. Pictures of the shuttle crew at meals usually show some down near the floor and some perched up near the ceiling. The people below don't have to worry about food dripping on their heads. If any food is spilled, it will just float in the air.

There are no squeeze tubes anymore. Astronauts use knives, forks, and spoons. Most foods are served in gravies or sauces to help them stick to the cutlery. But every drink needs a straw for sucking the liquid out. A drink won't pour out of a glass in space. Salt and pepper are in liquid form, because grains of salt would just float around instead of

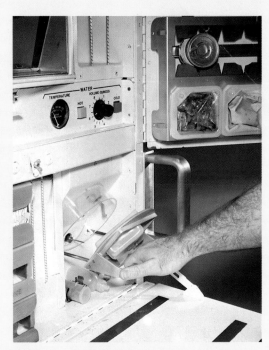

The crew take turns preparing food in the tiny orbiter kitchen.

falling onto the food. Sometimes the astronauts can't resist playing with their food. They spin it in the air and try to catch it in their mouths.

One of the best things about a meal in space is that you don't have to wash the dishes after-ward! The trays and cutlery are quickly wiped off with wet wipes and put away. Then all the food containers are collected and put in a big garbage bag that's sealed and taken back to Earth.

Dressing for Space

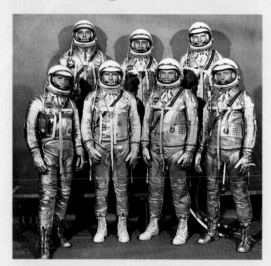

The Mercury spacesuit worn by the first NASA astronauts in 1959 was adapted from a high-altitude pressure suit.

Here are some instructions for putting on a pair of pants:
1. lift both your feet
2. pull your knees up against your stomach
3. hold the pants out from your body
4. push your feet down both pant legs at once.

Does this sound crazy? It makes perfect sense when you're weightless in space. If you try to put on one pant leg at a time, you'll probably find yourself turning somersaults!

Although getting into it might

be tricky, clothing for a shuttle flight is simple and comfortable. Because the crew compartment has an air supply and temperature controls, astronauts don't have to wear bulky space suits. Every astronaut has a pair of blue cotton long pants with a matching zippered jacket, blue cotton shorts, and a cotton knit short-sleeved shirt (usually navy blue, but some missions have worn other colors). These items come in standard sizes, and except for underwear, men and women wear the same clothing.

The astronauts don't wear shoes while they're in space, because they float from place to place rather than walk. Besides, a flailing foot with a hard shoe on it could injure someone. Sometimes the astronauts go barefoot and sometimes they wear socks with soft soles attached to them.

Although in-flight outfits look a lot like regular sports clothing, they're very carefully designed. The fabric is treated with chemicals to make it fireproof. The jacket has pleats in the shoulders and back to make it easier to move in, and also to make room for the astronauts to

Above: The busy work station at the rear of the flight deck on Discovery. *Judith Resnik has just unfolded the solar array panel shown on p. 34.*
Left: Wiley Post, shown here, developed the pressure suit in the 1930s so that airplane pilots could fly at high altitudes without blacking out. The rubber inflatable suit was worn over long underwear.

"grow" (weightless people stretch a couple of inches). Still, the clothing is close fitting enough that sleeves and pant legs can't catch on important equipment.

The jacket and pants are covered with a dozen pockets, closed with either Velcro strips or zippers. What goes in these pockets? Felt-tip pens and special ballpoint pens that can write in the weightlessness of the orbiter, pencils, notebooks, sunglasses for looking out the windows, a Swiss army pocketknife, and scissors (handy for opening plastic food packages). Most of these items have little strips of Velcro, so if they're put down for a moment, they won't float away.

There isn't much room to store personal belongings on the shuttle, so astronauts can't put on fresh clothing every day. The jacket, pants, and footwear have to do for the whole mission. They can change their shirts every three days, and their underwear every day.

On the day they return to Earth, the astronauts have to get back into the flight suits and shoes they wore for launch. (On her first mission, Sally Ride briefly

Close-up view of an astronaut in an EVA (space-walk) suit, ready to take a ride in space on an MMU (manned maneuvering unit).

mislaid her flight boots. Later she joked that she almost had to return from space in bare feet.) Once the first couple of test mis-

sions were completed, the shuttle crews of the early 1980s wore quite simple flight suits for launches and landings. When the

space-shuttle program resumed in 1988, after the *Challenger* tragedy, the escape hatch had been altered on the orbiter (see p. 10) so that astronauts could parachute out if there was an emergency. Now the astronauts leave and return to Earth in a pressurized suit with helmet, gloves and boots, and a parachute harness. This suit would provide a breathing system and protection from the cold, thin atmosphere at 20,000 feet (6,000 meters) if the astronauts had to eject. It could also keep them alive for up to 24 hours in a life raft if they had to ditch in the ocean.

Finally, each astronaut is issued a watch and earplugs and a sleep mask. ("Morning" comes every ninety minutes as the shuttle orbits the Earth, so the astronauts need a way to keep the light out of their eyes.)

The legs of the flight suit can be inflated during the flight back to Earth. G forces that build up during reentry cause blood to flow away from the head toward the legs. This could cause an astronaut to black out. The pressure of the inflated pants legs keeps this from happening.

Stepping Out

A "moon buggy", similar to this test vehicle on display at the Smithsonian, was first used on the moon during the Apollo 15 mission in 1971. Astronauts used it to explore and to gather moon rocks to bring back to Earth.

Fewer than 300 men and women have ever gone into space. And of these pioneers, fewer than 50 have made a space walk. Space is a hostile place for human beings. If you stepped out into the vacuum (airlessness) of space without a protective suit, your lungs would collapse. The side of your body facing the sun could be heated to 250° F (120° C), while the shady side of your body could be chilled to −150° F (−100° C). There's no atmosphere to shield you from the sun's harmful rays. Finally, although space seems empty, micrometeoroids whiz by from time to time. They're no bigger than grains of salt, but they can cause serious injury because they travel so fast.

If space is so dangerous, why not stay safe inside the spacecraft? In many cases it is worth the risk, because there is so much useful EVA work that astronauts can do. Way back in 1973 two space-walking astronauts saved the Skylab space station by freeing a jammed solar panel. In April 1984 astronauts James van Hoften and George Nelson repaired and redeployed the broken-down Solar Max satellite, worth $250 million. There have been several other satellite rescues and repairs since then.

Astronauts working outside the orbiter wear suits that are like personal spaceships, with everything they need to survive in space for a few hours. In the early days of the space program, astronauts wore custom-fitted space suits. Today's space suits come in several pieces. Each piece is available in various sizes, so that a suit can be put together to fit a person who is 5 feet 4 inches (160 centimeters) or 6 feet 2 inches (185 centimeters). The suit pieces can be reused and last for at least eight years.

Suppose you are an astronaut getting ready for an EVA. You start by putting on stretch underwear that looks like a set of white long johns with a zipper up the front. This special underwear has plastic tubing running through it. When you are working in space, cool water will run through these tubes to keep you from getting overheated. Next, you pull on the lower half of your bulky suit, pants and boots all in one piece. The upper half – a hard shell with movable arms – hangs on the airlock wall with its arms outstretched. You get into it by bending down under it and reaching up inside. The top and bottom half of the suit fit together with a metal ring joint. The upper half of the suit has a portable life-sup-

Astronauts James van Hoften (above) and George Nelson repair the Solar Max satellite in Challenger's *cargo bay.*

port system (PLSS) built right into it. The PLSS provides you with enough oxygen and electrical power for seven hours of EVA.

On your head you wear what the astronauts call a "Snoopy cap": a cloth cap with a headphone and microphone built in so you can communicate with your EVA partner, the orbiter, and with Mission Control. Over this you wear a bubble helmet. The final piece of the suit is a pair of heavy gloves with rubber fingertips to help you grip things.

When you're all suited up, you leave the space shuttle through the airlock, which can be closed off from the crew cabin. The airlock is depressurized (all its air is removed), and then you open the hatch. You attach your thin wire tether to the orbiter and float out into the blackness of space. While you're working in the cargo bay, you can use various handrails and pulleys to get from one place to

another. There are also footgrips that look like ski bindings. You can slide your feet into these to hold yourself in place while you work.

Work in space is very tiring. To make any kind of movement, you have to move parts of the bulky suit. Even opening and closing your hand takes effort. Fortunately, there's a water supply inside your suit with a straw near your mouth, so you can sip while working.

Six astronauts have taken the space-walk adventure even further. They've used manned maneuvering units (MMUs) to go as far as 320 feet (96 meters) from the orbiter, becoming human satellites of the Earth. The MMU looks like an armchair without legs. It is powered by 24 small jet thrusters that release spurts of nitrogen gas. The controls are on the two armrests. The right-hand control makes the MMU roll and lean forward, backward, and to the side. (For

example, James van Hoften used these controls to turn a slow somersault after completing his mission on Solar Max.) The left-hand control makes the MMU travel in a straight line. Mission specialist Joe Allen called the MMU "a three-dimensional flying carpet."

Above: *Astronaut Bruce McCandless takes the world's first untethered space walk in the MMU in February 1984.*

Above left: *Ed White, the first American to make a space walk, floats on a tether outside the spacecraft during the* Gemini 4 *mission in 1965.*

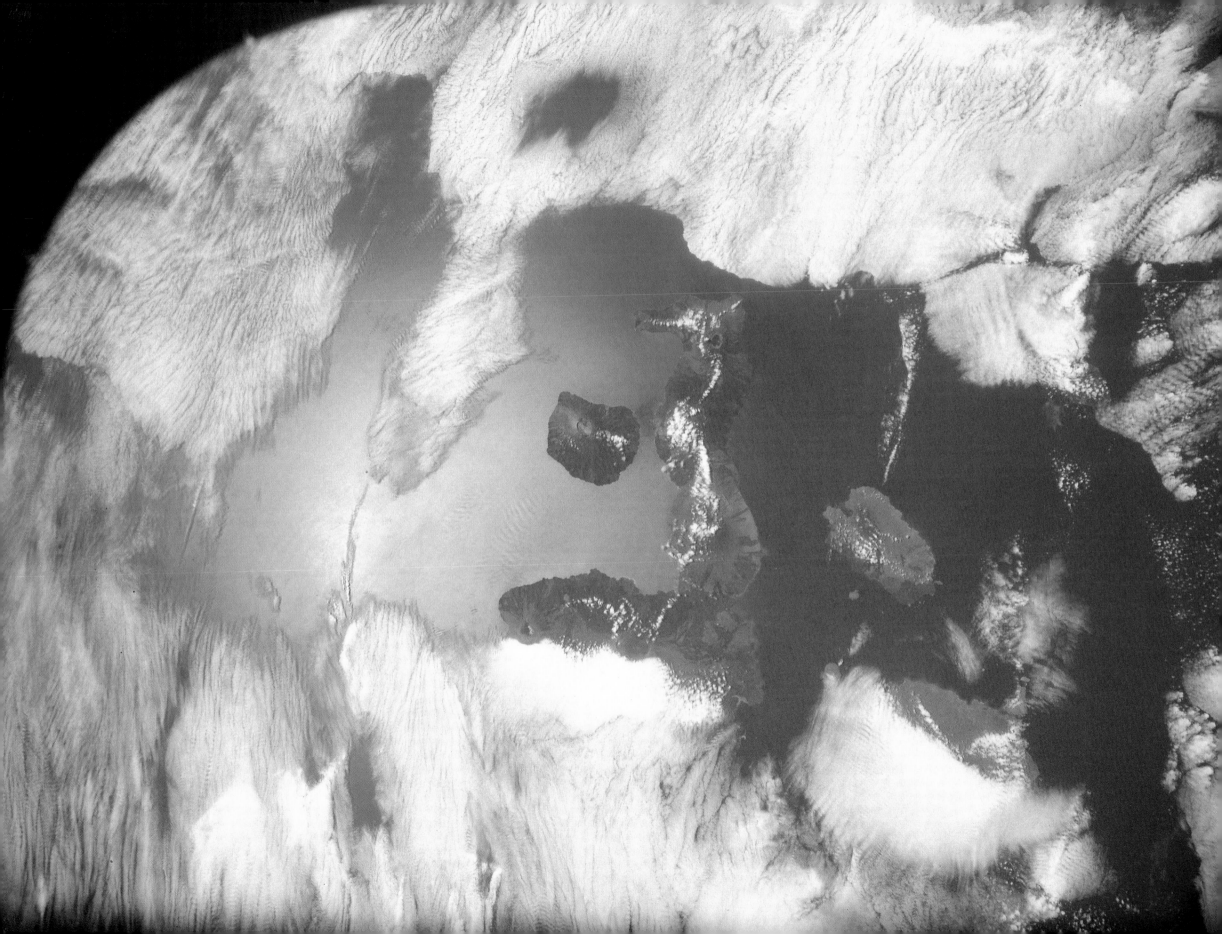

COMING HOME

The science experiments are all done and packed away, the satellite has been launched, and Kathryn Sullivan's space walk is already a part of space history. On the last full day of Mission 41G, the mission specialists and payload specialists have less exciting work to do: cleaning up the orbiter. All the books and other useful things that were attached to the walls and ceiling by Velcro strips have to be stowed away in lockers. Otherwise, as soon as the orbiter leaves its orbit, they'll all come crashing down on the astronauts' heads. Everyone fills big garbage bags with trash and stows them in a locker under the mid-deck floor. The astronauts try to be "good citizens of the universe" by bringing their trash back to Earth instead of dumping it in space.

Meanwhile, Commander Robert Crippen and Pilot Jon McBride are in their seats on the flight deck, checking over every part of the flight-control system they'll use to return from space tomorrow. Earlier in the week the astronauts had a clear view of Hurricane Josephine from the orbiter, and they wondered if this storm would keep them from landing in Florida. On two earlier missions

The age-old dream of traveling to outer space is shown in this fanciful 1638 illustration of a moon-flying machine.

Crippen had to land at Edwards Air Force Base in California because of bad weather at Cape Canaveral. He knows that California landings add a week to the tight shuttle schedule because the orbiter has to be "piggybacked" to Florida on top of a special 747 jet. Now he's happy to hear that everything looks good for a Florida landing at about noon the next day.

The next morning the astronauts find the flight suits and boots they wore for launch and put them on again. They drink lots of water – four or five glasses – and take some salt pills. While they've been weightless, their body tissues haven't held as much water as they would have back home. If the astronauts don't drink a lot beforehand, they'll feel very thirsty and dizzy when they feel Earth's gravity again.

The astronauts unpack and unfold the seats they will need for reentry and attach them to the floor. They close and lock the cargo bay doors using remote controls. Then they put on their helmets and strap themselves into their seats for the trip home. They're only 60 minutes away from a safe landing at the Kennedy Space Center in Florida.

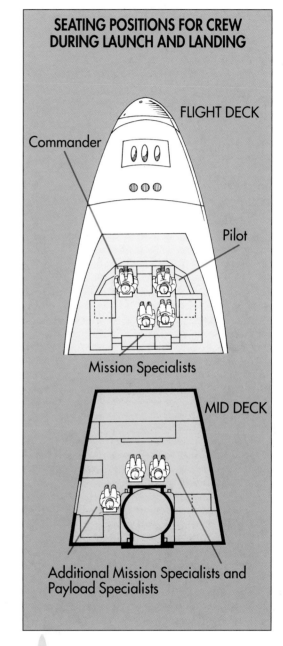

SEATING POSITIONS FOR CREW DURING LAUNCH AND LANDING

FLIGHT DECK

Commander

Pilot

Mission Specialists

MID DECK

Additional Mission Specialists and Payload Specialists

***Opposite page**: A view from the orbiter of the vast craters of the Galapagos Islands off the west coast of South America.*

Opposite page: An aerial view of the launch pad at Kennedy Space Center in Florida.

The orbiter has made 132 orbits of Earth and is now over Perth, Australia. Commander Crippen and Pilot McBride fire the small rocket engines of the orbiter's Reaction Control System (RCS) to turn the orbiter tailfirst in its orbit path. Then they fire the Orbital Maneuvering System (OMS) engines for about 2 minutes. This slows the orbiter by about 200 miles (320 kilometers) per hour – just enough to let Earth's gravity tug the orbiter out of orbit.

Then Commander Crippen fires the RCS engines again to put the orbiter in a nose-up position as it heads back toward Earth. About 30 minutes later the orbiter hits the thin outer reaches of the Earth's atmosphere, still traveling over 16,000 miles (over 26,000 kilometers) per hour.

A romantic nineteenth-century view of space travel in a balloon.

The closer to Earth the orbiter gets, the thicker the atmosphere gets. The air rubs hard against the orbiter and slows it down. This rubbing, or friction, causes intense heat – the nosecap and the leading edges of the wings can heat up to 3,000° F (1650° C). If it weren't for the special tiles and carbon material protecting the outside of the orbiter (see p. 22), it would burn up. The crew cabin stays at its usual comfortable temperature, but an eerie orange light floods through the windows as the orbiter glows red-hot. Commander Crippen, who has been through this three times before, reminds the first-timers that the glow is normal.

The heated air around the orbiter blocks out normal communication from Earth for the next 15 minutes or so. The astronauts can hear wind whistling around the orbiter as it hurtles down through the

---

KATHRYN DWYER SULLIVAN

Born Paterson, New Jersey, October 3, 1951

Only two women have ever walked in space – Svetlana Savitskaya of the Soviet Union and Kathryn Sullivan. Sullivan's turn came on Mission 41G of *Challenger*, on October 11, 1984. She and David Leestma tested a satellite refueling system that may someday be used to give orbiting satellites a longer life.

Sally Ride was also aboard on Mission 41G, on her second spaceflight. Sullivan and Ride had an unusual connection – they had been in the same first-grade class, although they never saw each other again until they started astronaut training together.

Sullivan worked hard for several years to prepare for her next mission – the launch of the mighty Hubble Space Telescope. Not only did the shuttle put the telescope into orbit, but later missions will maintain and repair it. Sullivan helped develop a set of 96 special tools used on the telescope. She has spent long hours in a water tank practicing "weightless" repair work on the telescope to get ready for her next space walk.

"I don't want to be an astronaut just because we mucked up down here and need to run away from the mess," Sullivan says. "Space exploration works as long as it's not a substitute for taking care of the Earth."

Above: Artist Miriam Schottland's fantasy painting, "The Spectators," shows alligators and other Florida wildlife watching a shuttle launch.

Opposite page: Discovery, returning from its maiden voyage of 2.17 million miles (3.5 million kilometers), landed on the extra-long runway at Edwards Air Force Base in California.

atmosphere. The sound starts as a soft whisper and builds to a shriek.

The G forces build up, making the astronauts feel about one and a half times heavier than they do on Earth. This is less than the 3 Gs they felt when they launched, but it bothers them more now because they've been weightless for longer than a week. On the way up the astronauts were lying on their backs, so the G forces pushed against their chests. On the way back they are in a sitting position, and the G forces push the blood out of their heads and down toward their feet. To keep from blacking out, some

of the crew wear "G suits," which are inflatable pants. When they are blown up, the pants press on the astronauts' legs and keep the blood from gathering there.

The closer the orbiter gets to Earth, the less it acts like a spacecraft, and the more it acts like a glider. The commander can also control a rudder in the tall vertical tail, which can be used as a speed brake, and a large movable flap under the rear engines to change the orbiter's position. To slow the orbiter down, the commander takes it through some big S-shaped turns.

At 12 minutes to touchdown, the orbiter comes out of its blackout. It's still 34 miles (54 kilometers) above Earth and traveling 8,300 miles (13,000 kilometers) per hour. The orbiter has crossed the coast of Alaska and is heading southeast across North America, passing over Winnipeg, Milwaukee, Indianapolis, Knoxville, Atlanta....

With just over 5 minutes to touchdown, the orbiter is still 16 miles (26 kilometers) above the Earth and going 1,700 miles (2,700 kilometers) per hour. At 3 minutes to touchdown, the orbiter slows to the speed of sound, and thousands of people waiting on the ground hear a thundering sonic boom.

Commander Crippen makes a wide left turn to line up the orbiter with the runway. The final approach to the runway has to be exactly right – the orbiter has no engines to take it up to try the approach again. The orbiter comes in on a much steeper path, and much faster, than a jet passenger plane. The astronauts hang forward in their shoulder harnesses, feeling as if they're headed straight down. The landing gear comes down just a few seconds before touchdown. The wheels of the main landing gear hit the

runway, giving off a small puff of smoke. Then the nose wheel comes down with a heavier jolt. The crew members know they have made a safe landing.

The commander and pilot put on the wheel brakes to bring the orbiter to a safe stop. Fortunately the runway at the Kennedy Space Center is 15,000 feet (4,600 meters) long – about one and a half times the length of a regular airport runway.

The runway, like the launchpad, is surrounded by Florida swampland. Commander Crippen likes to joke that NASA put the landing strip in the middle of alligator-filled water to encourage pilots not to overshoot the runway! In fact, alligators sometimes turn up on the runway too. Heated by the sun during the day, the runway stays warm at night, so the alligators like to sleep on it. On mornings when an orbiter is due back, Kennedy Space Center staff make sure the alligators are out of the way.

A ground crew quickly surrounds the orbiter. They are wearing heavy protective suits and they have special equipment to test for any poisonous or explosive gases leaking from the orbiter. If they detect any problems, there will be a quick emergency evacuation for the crew. But all is well. A passenger staircase like the ones airlines use is rolled up to the side of the orbiter. A doctor bounds up the steps first to give the crew a quick checkup.

The astronauts, feeling a little dazed, have already unstrapped themselves from their seats. Just an hour ago they could float from the flight deck to the mid deck. Now they have to climb down a ladder to the mid deck, feeling as if lead weights are attached to their boots. Their hearts aren't used to pumping blood against the pull of gravity, and the astronauts feel their pulses racing as they do a few knee bends and practice walking for the first time in a week.

Finally, about 30 minutes after landing, the astronauts step out into the Florida sunlight. They're happy and relieved that their mission went well and that they're home safely. Still, they can't help feeling sorry the adventure is over. As Kathryn Sullivan put it after Mission 41G, "I'd like to fly every flight we have on the schedule! Life will never be like that, of course. I have spent ten years with NASA and eight and a half days in space. That's not unusual."

Opposite page: If the orbiter lands in California, it travels piggyback on a special NASA 747 to Florida so that it can be launched again.

Below: Another mission ends safely as the orbiter touches down at the Kennedy Space Center in Florida.

Great Achievements in Spaceflight

All dates are launch dates.

Sputnik 1 (USSR) Oct. 4, 1957. Unmanned. The first satellite to be put into orbit.

Sputnik 2 (USSR) Nov. 2, 1957. Unmanned – dog **Laika** aboard. First living creature to orbit the Earth – survived 10 days in space but could not be returned to Earth.

2.

Vostok 1 (USSR) Apr. 12, 1961. **Yuri Gagarin** – first human being in space – 1 orbit of Earth lasting 1 hour 48 minutes.

5.

Mercury 3 (USA) May 5, 1961. **Alan Shepard** – first American in space – suborbital flight lasting 15 minutes.

1.

Mercury 6 (USA) Feb. 20, 1962. **John Glenn** – first American in orbit – 3 orbits, lasting 4 hours 55 minutes.

3.

Vostok 6 (USSR) June 6, 1963. **Valentina Tereshkova** – first woman in space – 3-day mission.

4.

Voskhod 1 (USSR) Oct. 12, 1964. **Vladimir Komarov, Boris Yegorov, Konstantin Feoktisov** – first spaceflight with more than one person aboard.

Voskhod 2 (USSR) Mar. 18, 1965. **Pavel Balyayev, Alexei Leonov** – first space walk, by Leonov – 10 minutes.

6.

7.

Gemini 4 (USA) June 3, 1965. **James McDivitt, Edward White** – first U.S. space walk, by White – 21 minutes.

Gemini 8 (USA) Mar. 16, 1966. **Neil Armstrong, David Scott** – first docking in space, with an unmanned Agena Target Vehicle.

8.

Apollo 8 (USA) Dec. 21, 1968. **Frank Borman, James Lovell, William Anders** – first manned spacecraft to go around the moon.

9.

Soyuz 4 (USSR) Jan. 14, 1969. **Vladimir Shatalov.**

Soyuz 5 (USSR) Jan. 15, 1969. **Boris Volyanov, Yevgeny Khrunov, Alexei Yeleseyev** – first docking of two manned vehicles; first transfer of people from one vehicle to another.

10.

Apollo 11 (USA) July 16, 1969. **Neil Armstrong**, **Michael Collins**, **Edwin Aldrin**. While Collins pilots command module, Armstrong (followed by Aldrin) is the first human being to set foot on the moon.

11.

FIRST MAN ON THE MOON

Apollo 18 (USA) July 15, 1975. **Thomas Stafford**, **Vance Brand**, **Donald Slayton** *Soyuz 19* (USSR). **Alexei Leonov**, **Valery Kubasov** – first U.S. - Soviet docking in space; spacecraft remained docked for two days, with crews visiting back and forth.

12.

Columbia (USA) *STS-1* Apr. 12, 1981. **John Young**, **Robert Crippen** – first space shuttle mission.

Challenger (USA) *STS-7* June 18, 1983. **Robert Crippen**, **Frederick Hauck**, **Sally Ride**, **John Fabian**, **Norman Thagard**, – first American woman in space, Sally Ride.

Challenger (USA) *STS-10, Mission 41B* Feb. 3, 1984. **Vance Brand**, **Robert Gibson**, **Bruce McCandless**, **Ronald McNair**, **Robert Stewart** – first free-floating space walk using manned maneuvering unit (MMU) by McCandless.

Soyuz T-12 (USSR) July 17, 1984. **Vladimir Dzhanibekov**, **Svetlana Savitskaya**, **Igor Volk** – first space walk by a woman, Savitskaya.

Challenger (USA) *STS-13, Mission 41G* Oct. 5, 1984. **Robert Crippen**, **Jon McBride**, **Sally Ride**, **Kathryn Sullivan**, **David Leestma**, **Marc Garneau**,

13.

UNITED STATES IN SPACE · · · A DECADE OF ACHIEVEMENT

14.

Paul Scully-Power – first space walk by an American woman, Sullivan; first Canadian in space, Garneau.

Soyuz TM-4 (USSR) Dec. 21, 1987. **Vladimir Titov**, **Musa Manarov**, **Anatoly Levchenko** – space endurance record for Titov and Manarov – stayed at Mir space station for 366 days; returned to Earth on *Soyuz TM-6*.

Discovery (USA) *STS-31* Apr. 24, 1990. **Loren Shriver**, **Charles Bolden**, **Steven Hawley**, **Bruce McCandless**, **Kathryn Sullivan** – launch of first telescope to view the universe from outside Earth's atmosphere – the Hubble Space Telescope.

Postage stamps shown in this chart
Page 58
1. *Laika and the launch tower – Poland*
2. *Yuri Gagarin – Poland*
3. *Valentina Tereshkova – USSR*
4. *Voskhod 1 – Bulgaria*
5. *Project Mercury – U.S.A.*
6. *Voskhod 2 – Romania*
7. *Edward White's spacewalk – Nicaragua*
8. *Gemini 8 – Romania*
9. *Apollo 8 – USA*
10. *Soyuz 4 and 5 crew – USSR*
Page 59
11. *Apollo 11, Neil Armstrong – USA*
12. *Thomas Stafford – Jordan*
13. *Apollo 15, first use of lunar rover – USA*
14. *Block of space achievement stamps including space shuttle – USA*

HOW THE ORBITERS GOT THEIR NAMES

Gustave Doré, a famous nineteenth-century French engraver, created this dreamlike picture of a sailing ship floating up to the moon. In the tradition of the great seafaring explorers of the past, NASA names its orbiters for famous sailing ships.

The Enterprise, completed in 1976, was named for Captain Kirk's ship in the popular TV series *Star Trek*. Fans were very disappointed when they found out that the name had been given to a test model that was never designed to fly in space.

Columbia, which made the first shuttle flight in April 1981, was named for a U.S. Navy frigate that sailed all the way around the world in 1836, and also for the command module for the first moon landing in July 1969.

Challenger, launched for the first time in April 1983, was named for a U.S. Navy ship that explored the Atlantic and Pacific oceans in the 1870s. (*Challenger* was also the name of the Apollo 17 lunar module on the last mission to the moon in 1972.)

Discovery, launched for the first time in August 1984, was named for the ships of two famous explorers. Henry Hudson explored Hudson Bay in 1610–1611 while sailing on a ship called *Discovery*. A different *Discovery* took part in James Cook's voyage to the Hawaiian Islands in 1776.

Atlantis, launched for the first time in October 1985, was named for an American two-masted ketch that sailed more than 500,000 miles (more than 800,000 kilometers) between 1930 and 1936, carrying out oceanographic research.

During 1988 NASA ran a contest for American students to name an orbiter under construction. Over 71,000 young people entered, in two contest divisions: Kindergarten to Grade 6 and Grade 7 to Grade 12. The winning name was *Endeavour*. This was the name of Captain James Cook's flagship on his first voyage to the South Pacific in 1768–1772, when he charted New Zealand and explored the eastern coastline of Australia. The winning students were a fifth-grade class from Senatobia, Mississippi and an eighth-to-twelfth-grade team from Tallulah Falls, Georgia. The name *Endeavour* was a very popular entry in the contest, but these students won for the quality of their projects to explain the name choice.

The Space Shuttle Discovery.

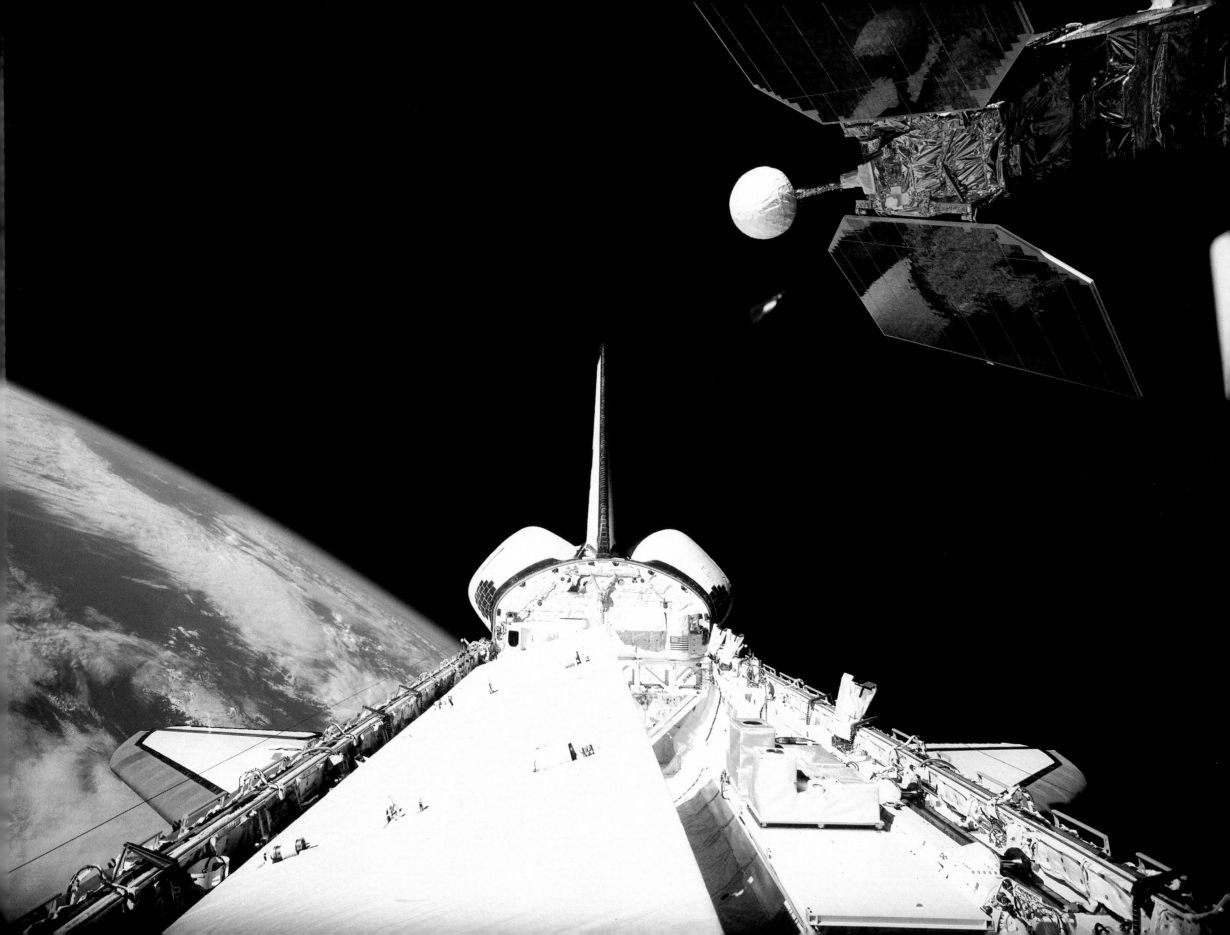

CREDITS

SI	Smithsonian Institution
NASM	National Air and Space Museum
NMAH	National Museum of American History
L	Left
R	Right
T	Top
B	Bottom

Photographs from the film *The Dream Is Alive*, distributed by Imax Systems Corporation:

Front and back cover, title page, contents page, and pages *i*, **4, 7, 9, 11, 13, 15, 17** L, **19, 20, 23, 25, 27, 29, 30, 31, 32, 33, 34, 37, 39, 40, 41, 42** R, **43, 44, 46**T, **50, 53, 55, 56, 57, 61, 62.**

Photographs from the Smithsonian Institution

Page 5 – SI/NASM. Illustration from Jules Verne, *From the Earth to the Moon ... and a Trip around It* (New York: Scribner, Armstrong & Co., 1874).
Page 12 – SI/NASM
Page 14 R – SI/NASM
Page 18 – SI/NASM. Illustration from Jules Verne, *From the Earth to the Moon ... and a Trip around It* (New York: Scribner, Armstrong & Co., 1874).
Page 38 – SI/NASM. Illustration from Jules Verne, *From the Earth to the Moon ... and a Trip around It* (New York: Scribner, Armstrong & Co., 1874).
Page 46 B – SI/NASM
Page 48 L – SI/NASM
Page 51 L – SI/NASM. Modern rendition by Bernard Brussel-Smith of an illustration that originally appeared in Bishop Francis Godwin's *The Man in the Moone, or A Discourse Thither by Domingo Gonsales The Speedy Messenger* (London, 1638).
Page 52 R – SI/NASM
Pages 58-59 – SI/NMAH/National Philatelic Collection
Page 60 L – SI/NASM. Gustave Doré (1832 – 1883), French edition of *The Singular Travels, Campaigns, and Adventures of Baron Munchausen* (Paris, 1862).

Photographs from the National Aeronautics and Space Administration / NASA:

Pages 6, 8 R, **10, 14** L, **16, 17**R, **24, 26**TL, **28**R, **42**L, **45**L, **45**R, **46**L, **47, 48**R, **49**L, **49**R, **52**L, **60**R, **63**.
Page 35 – *Space Flight Evolution*, an artist's conception of the evolution of manned space flight / Courtesy of Rockwell International.
Page 54 – Courtesy NASA Art Program Collection / *The Spectators*, painting by Miriam Schottland.

Above *: An astronaut uses a manned maneuvering unit (MMU) to make a short trip away from the orbiter.*

Page 61 photograph*: The ERBS satellite, deployed by Sally Ride on Mission 41G, floats free of the orbiter's cargo bay. This satellite was designed to measure how much heat the Earth receives from the sun, and how much of this heat it retains.*

Page 62 photograph*: "Now that we know how to live and work in space, we stand at the threshold of a new age of discovery."*
These are the last words of the film script for The Dream Is Alive.

INDEX